BACH
and his world

BACH

and his world

BY WERNER NEUMANN

THAMES AND HUDSON · LONDON

This edition © Thames and Hudson 1961
Revised edition 1969
Translated by Stefan de Haan
from Bach, Eine Bildbiographie
© Kindler Verlag Munich
Printed in Austria
500 13028 0

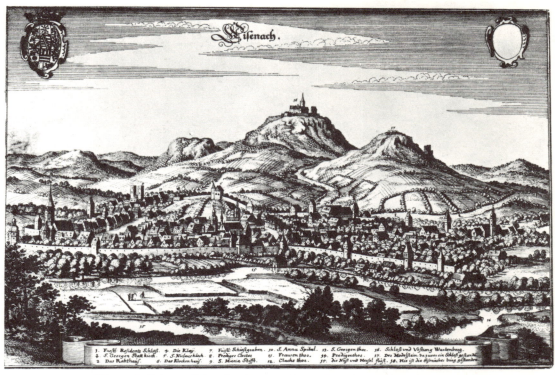

Eisenach, Johann Sebastian Bach's place of birth in the 17th century

THE NAME OF BACH has come to be associated with a unique family tradition in music. The family, which is Thuringian, can be traced back to the Reformation. They survived the Thirty Years' War and spread far afield during the seventeenth and eighteenth centuries. All over the country musically gifted members of the family were given important positions as town pipers, organists or precentors. The determination to improve their social position by means of a professional discipline is unmistakable, and the incidence of members of the Bach family among musicians in Thuringia led in the end to the popular habit of substituting the name 'Bach' for the definition 'musician'.

Erfurt, Arnstadt, Eisenach as well as Jena, Mühlhausen, Ohrdruf, Gehren and Meiningen were the centres of this development. Amongst them, Eisenach became the focal point during the last decades of the seventeenth century because Johann Christoph, the most gifted Bach before Johann Sebastian, was

Johann Ambrosius Bach (1645–95),
Johann Sebastian's father

organist at the Georgenkirche in that town. In the annals of the family he is described as 'the great and expressive composer'.

The fact that Johann Sebastian's name is also connected with this town is due to the stubborn town councillors who prevented their reliable court and town musician Johann Ambrosius Bach from accepting an engagement elsewhere; for, in 1684, after twelve years of service, he was invited to return to a better position in his home town Erfurt where he had been previously employed as musician to the council. There, in 1668, he had married Elisabeth Lämmerhirt, a furrier's daughter, and three years later the couple moved to Eisenach.

Birth The eighth child of this marriage was a son, born March 21, 1685 and christened Johann Sebastian two days later in the Georgenkirche. There are no records of his early years, and there is still some doubt whether he was actually born in the spacious and stately town house at the Frauenplan. This building, which is generally assumed to have belonged to the Bach family, was taken over in 1906 and restored with care by the new Bach Gesellschaft. It is among the most beautiful of the houses of famous men in Germany, as well proportioned as it is restful.

The 'Bach House' in Eisenach.
Below: Entry of Johann Sebastian's baptism in the church register on March 23, 1685

It is likely that Johann Sebastian learnt to play the violin and cembalo at an early age in his father's house; what is even more likely is that his famous uncle Johann Christoph Bach initiated him into the art of organ-playing. From his eighth year onwards he went to the old Latin school, where Martin Luther had been a pupil before him.

When he was nine years of age two sad events changed the course of his young life: both his mother and his father died, within nine months of each other. Johann Sebastian and Johann Jakob were taken into the house of their eldest brother Johann Christoph, who had recently married and now held the post of organist at the Michaeliskirche at Ohrdruf.

For Johann Sebastian this move from Eisenach to Ohrdruf was decisive. He left the world of town pipers for that of the church musician, and with his untiring zeal for learning he soon felt at home in his new surroundings. In a short time 'he had mastered all the pieces his brother had voluntarily given

The organ of the Georgenkirche
in Eisenach designed
by Johann Christoph Bach
(only the screen has survived)

The courtyard of the Dominican monastery in Eisenach where Bach went to school

him', and in this brother, a former pupil of the famous Pachelbel, he found an excellent teacher. Progress, however, seemed slow and laborious to the young Johann Sebastian. The first, and trustworthy, account of his life, the 'Nekrolog' by Carl Philipp Emanuel Bach and Johann Friedrich Agricola, reports concerning this period:

'A book of clavier pieces by famous contemporary masters such as Froberger, Kerll and Pachelbel was for some unknown reason withheld from the young boy, in spite of all his pleading. His constant desire to improve himself prompted him to the following innocent deception. His brother kept the book in a cupboard which had only bars for a door. At night, when everyone was asleep, he was able to force his little hands through the bars, roll up the paper-bound book, and pull it out. He then proceeded to copy it, by moonlight, as he did not even

The Michaeliskirche in Ohrdruf

Ohrdruf in the 18th century

have a candle. In six months he had made this treasure of music his own. Secretly and with great determination he set about making good use of it when to his great distress his brother discovered what had happened. The copy made with so much diligence was confiscated without compunction. The distress of a miser whose ship had foundered with a hundred thousand silver pieces on the voyage to Peru, might serve to illustrate the grief this loss brought to the little Johann Sebastian.'

During this period he went to school at the distinguished Gymnasium (High School) of Ohrdruf where he was taught according to the reformed educational principles of Comenius. Though Johann Sebastian held honourable positions in the school register and reached the top form at an exceptionally early age, he left school prematurely when he was fifteen years old. The growing number of children made his brother's house too small. A Latin entry in the school register made by the headmaster, states that Bach, unable to obtain a free place at the school, had gone to Lüneburg on March 15, 1700. The wealthy Michaelis monastery in this town was known to offer to poor boys with musical talent a secure existence in the choir, especially if they happened to come from Thuringia where singing was the popular pastime. The precentor of Ohrdruf, Elias Herda, who had himself held a scholarship there, may well have been the mediator.

Choirboy at Lüneburg

Together with a school-friend, Georg Erdmann, of whom we shall hear again, the young Bach set out on his journey of a hundred and eighty miles to this

The town of Lüneburg after a 17th-century engraving

musical centre of North Germany, where 'he was well received because of his uncommonly beautiful soprano voice'. The names of both boys figured in the list of remunerations for the choir as from April 3, which means that they must have arrived in Lüneburg just in time to take part in the solemn Easter music. As a singer, Bach now came to know the choral works of the great masters who had composed in the *a cappella* style, and, so fascinated was he by their skilful interweaving of polyphonic voices that he remained forever indebted to them in the writing of his own choral compositions. Moreover, he also learned a good deal from contemporary works of church music written in the *concertante* style. When his beautiful soprano voice broke he continued to be useful at performances as an accomplished violinist or organist.

A page in the register of the Ohrdruf Gymnasium. The second name in both columns is that of J. S. Bach, and in the lower group it is followed by a note on his departure for Lüneburg

An account of payments made to choristers of the Michaelisschule in Lüneburg. Bach was a member from 1700 to 1702; his name is ninth on the list

Interior of the Michaeliskirche in Lüneburg

It was his good fortune that in Georg Böhm, the organist of the Johannis-kirche, he met a fellow-countryman from the neighbourhood of Ohrdruf and a friend of the Bach family. Böhm, a pupil of the Hamburg organist Jan Adams Reinken, introduced him to the great organ traditions of Hamburg. The influence of the Lüneburg master is evident in Bach's organ partitas as well as in some other early compositions for the organ, and it is likely that, on his advice, Bach undertook repeated journeys to Hamburg, the town of organs and

Jan Adams Reinken,
famous organist of the
Katharinenkirche in Hamburg

organists — in particular to hear Jan Adams Reinken in the Katharinenkirche.

His close contact with the French cultural sphere was important for the development of his instrumental style. The proximity of the old Michaelis school to the modern academy for young aristocrats made it easy to introduce Bach to the French style of life and education prevailing at that institute, and the talented French *maître de dance* Thomas de la Selle, a pupil of Lully's, acquainted him with the music of his own country. He probably also introduced the young

Bach, by virtue of his astonishing proficiency in violin playing, to the court of Celle, where, at the same time, he was employed as a musician. The court was presided over by a vivacious duke and a duchess of noble French ancestry, and between them they had created a miniature Versailles. The excellent French orchestra with its rhythmic and elegant way of playing must have made a profound impression on Bach. He copied many clavier and organ pieces by French composers in order to master their style. His inclination towards this type of music, evident in his later instrumental works, has its origin in these early experiences at Celle. The happy combination of educational and cultural opportunities allowed him to widen his horizon both as a man and as an artist, thus making his stay at Lüneburg a profitable one. This would hardly have been possible with the limitations of the small Thuringian towns, yet soon he began once more to turn towards his home ground.

An organ which greatly interested Bach was under construction at the new church of Arnstadt. Besides, members of his family had been professionally

In 1703 Bach became organist of the Neue Kirche in Arnstadt (below). Before he could start work at Arnstadt Bach had the opportunity of studying the French style of music at the palace of Celle (right)

active in this district for four generations, and because of this the chances of finding employment there looked promising.

Bach's biographer Forkel has given a vivid and amusing account, based on information supplied by the composer's two eldest sons, illustrating the community sense and the feeling of mutual attachment common to all whose name was Bach:

'Since it was impossible that they should all live in the same town, yet wanted to meet at least once a year, they decided upon a certain day on which everyone had to be present at a place previously agreed upon. This practice continued even when the number of family members had greatly increased and spread across the frontiers of Thuringia into Upper and Lower Saxony as well as into Franconia. The place chosen for this convention was usually Erfurt, Eisenach or Arnstadt. Since the gathering consisted purely of organists, precentors and town musicians, who were all connected with the Church in one way or another, the convention was opened with the singing of a chorale, as was the custom in those times when all proceedings were ushered in by an act of devotion. After this pious introduction they passed on to some lighter entertainment which often enough provided rather a contrast to the former, as they now began to sing folksongs, some funny, some even frivolous; and they all sang together, extemporizing in such a way that the voices made up a kind of harmony while the words were different in each part. This kind of improvised ensemble they used to call Quodlibet . . .'

The motive for his return to Thuringia in 1702 was the wish to be closer to his family, as well as the hope of being appointed organist with an instrument of his own. Since the completion of the Arnstadt organ was delayed until 1703, Bach accepted the interim position of violinist in the small chamber orchestra of Duke Johann Ernst of Sachsen-Weimar. As deputy for the old court organist Effler he was also able to practise his beloved art of organ-playing.

In 1703, during the month of July, the council of Arnstadt honoured the eighteen-year-old Bach by inviting him to test the finished organ, which he did to everyone's satisfaction. He then impressed the people of Arnstadt so much *Organist at* with his playing during the dedication of the instrument that he was offered *Arnstadt* the post of organist on the most favourable terms. Having signed the contract on August 9, 1703, he returned to Weimar and after a short time he took up his new position.

At last Bach had his own organ, a small but well equipped instrument, and with great enthusiasm he set to work on perfecting his playing technique and his style of composition. Instinctively he chose the best composers as models, and the 'Nekrolog' reports at length on this subject: 'Now for the first time he began to reap the benefits of his untiring efforts to become an accomplished organist and composer. He had acquired his knowledge and technique mostly by studying the best works of famous contemporary musicians, and by applying his own mind to the problems involved. His models were Bruhns, Reinken, Buxtehude and a few good French organists.'

He even paid a personal visit to Dietrich Buxtehude, the most important organist of the North German School, having first applied on October 1705 to his ecclesiastical council for permission to go to Lübeck and to absent himself

for four weeks. Moved by the music he heard at the 'Musical Evenings' in the Marienkirche and fascinated by the discussions with the master about the arts, he stayed on for three months without having his leave of absence extended. It was February before he returned, the richer for his experiences and with plans for the future.

The people of Arnstadt soon became aware of the effect this pilgrimage was having on their organist. Not only did his new-fangled musical ideas bewilder and surprise the congregation, but they caused some real confusion during the communal singing. One cannot blame the traditionally-minded church council for summoning their impetuous organist on February 21, 1706 and reprimanding him for the 'many odd variations' and 'strange sounds' for which he was respon-

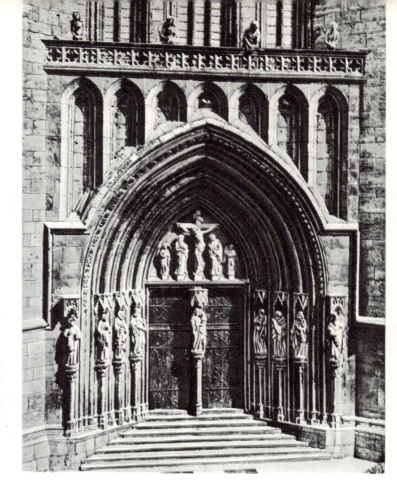

Bach acknowledges the receipt of 18 florins on June 15, 1707 to the church authorities at Arnstadt

The cantata *Gott ist mein König* for the inauguration of the new council was performed on February 4, 1708, in the Marienkirche in Mühlhausen

sible. At the same time he was asked to explain the unauthorized extension of his leave. Bach's proud and provocative answers were not exactly suited for self-justification nor to pour oil on troubled waters; nevertheless, the authorities continued to treat their young organist with leniency.

But soon new conflicts arose. Despite repeated admonitions Bach refused to work with the undisciplined boys' choir, pointing out that under his contract he was not bound to do so. In the course of a further meeting of the council on November 11, 1706 he was once more reproached, but no more than the evasive promise of a written statement could be extracted from him. The further reproach that he had permitted a 'strange damsel' to take part in the church music is interesting not only in relation to this particular performance: the lady in

In 1707 Johann Sebastian married his cousin Maria Barbara in the village church at
Dornheim

question was probably Bach's own cousin Maria Barbara, his future wife. Apart
from these authenticated differences of opinion with the council to whom he
was responsible, there may well have been other incidents in the course of his
duties which caused him to look elsewhere for a new field of activity.

During the latter part of 1706 he heard that the organist to the town of
Mühlhausen on the river Unstrut, one Johann Georg Ahle, had died. Presumably Bach had visited this free city on his journeys to North Germany; perhaps
he had even gathered impressions of the long-established and abundant musical
activities there. As early as the sixteenth century Joachim a Burck had made
important contributions to church and school music in this town, and his pupil

Johannes Eccard became a highly esteemed master of the sacred and secular song. A little later in the seventeenth century, the fame of the organist and composer Johann Rudolf Ahle spread far beyond his home town and he was given the unusual honour of being nominated to the council, and becoming Mayor of Mühlhausen. His son and successor as organist to the Blasiuskirche, Johann Georg, even received a crown of imperial laurel as a distinction for his achievements as poet and composer.

It is understandable therefore that Bach regarded the prospect of being organist at the Blasiuskirche as a tempting proposition. It is also probable that the council of Mühlhausen approached him, as serious negotiations were soon under way. The audition was fixed for Easter Sunday of the year 1707.

The artistry of the young organist so impressed the gentlemen of the council that they gladly conceded all his demands which, although not exceeding his modest income at Armstadt, were a good deal more ambitious than those of his predecessor. The contract was signed on June 15 and assured the newly appointed organist of 85 florins per annum, 450 litres of grain, 256 cubic feet of beech and oak wood and thirty dozen bundles of firewood to be delivered to his door. In return he promised to attend to his church duties and music with 'dedication and zeal', to take good care of 'the organ entrusted to him', to be of 'faithful and gracious' disposition towards the town council, to be of 'good and decent behaviour' and to avoid 'bad and suspicious company'. *Organist at Mühlhausen*

It was easy to obtain his release from the council at Arnstadt after the new contract had been signed. There is an entry in the records saying that Bach 'had returned the keys of his office to the council'. A carriage arrived one day in the late summer from Mühlhausen and took the renegade with his few belongings and many ideas towards his new environment.

The aspect of the free city of Mühlhausen was by no means inviting: a devastating fire had, only a few months earlier, destroyed a quarter of the entire inhabited area. The damage was particularly bad in the parish of St Blasius. Bach had therefore to face various hardships both in his professional capacity and of a private nature. The high rent he had to pay for his house, which caused him to complain later, may perhaps be attributed to the disaster.

Unfortunately nothing is known about his dwellings in Mühlhausen. He remained a bachelor for only a short period before rescuing his lonely cousin from her solitude at Arnstadt. Maria Barbara herself came from a musical family. She was the youngest daughter of Johann Michael Bach, the organist at Gehren. The marriage between her and Johann Sebastian was celebrated on October 17, 1707, in the little village church of Dornheim, not far from Mühlhausen, where a friend, the vicar Lorenz Stauber, conducted the ceremony. The couple were to have eight children, among them the highly talented sons Wilhelm Friedemann, Philipp Emanuel and Gottfried Bernhard, and the strong unity within this family was for Bach a source of creative power as long as he lived.

In the contract little is said about his proposed artistic activities at Mühlhausen. The young and fiery musician had in any case the highest goals in view. He intended to raise the spiritual level of church music in general. Citizens and council were known to have some artistic sense, but their tastes were kept by Bach's predecessors within the modest limits of simple songs and arias. It was necessary therefore to begin to put new ideas into effect by 'collecting, that is to say, copying—and not without expense', a sizeable stock of carefully selected church music, by organizing an accomplished church choir and by establishing a good orchestra. Bach even found time to give his attention to the city's environs and be of assistance in matters of 'church music which was on the increase in almost every village'.

The result of these efforts became evident at the festive inauguration of the new council in February 1708. Such splendour as accompanied the performance of Johann Sebastian's cantata 'Gott ist mein König' in the spacious Marienkirche had hitherto been unheard of in Mühlhausen. The orchestra was sub-

 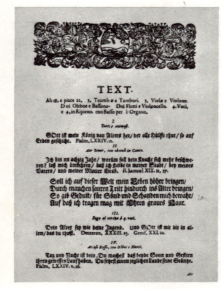

Left: Title page and opening text of the cantata *Gott ist mein König*, composed for the inauguration of the new Mühlhausen council.

Right: The last bars in the autograph score

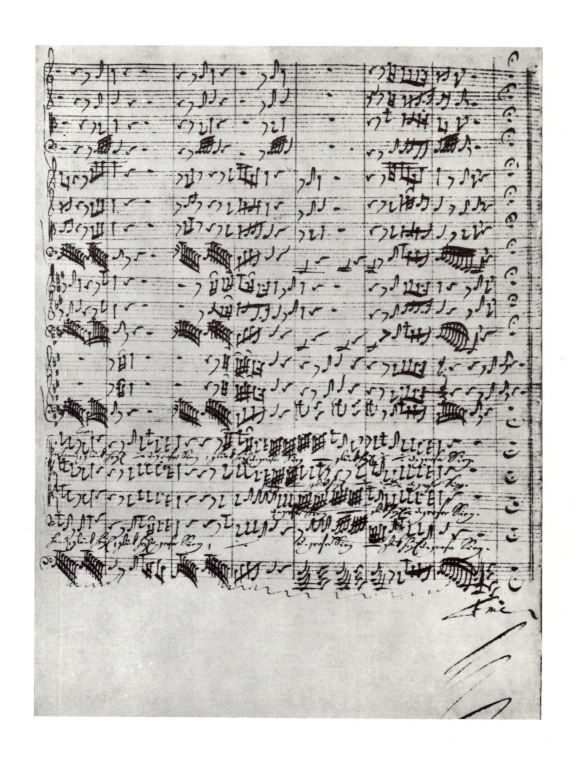

25

divided into four sections and the choir parts were manifold and varied. The style of this work based on chorales, words from the Bible and some verses of dedication, combined old and new ideas, but the development of the choral fugues in particular showed that he was far ahead of his time. The fact that the council authorized the publication of the material used in this performance is probably due more to vanity than to a recognition of the composer's merits. (Incidentally this is the only surviving cantata which was printed during Bach's lifetime.)

His great success gave Bach the courage to demand a complete renovation of the organ at the St Blasiuskirche. It is interesting to note that his detailed project, listing eleven points, included a carillon of twenty-six bells. It showed the young man also in other ways to be an expert on organ-building technique, and as such he was henceforth known in professional circles. The proposed plan was accepted by the council without reservation and the established organ-builder Johann Friedrich Wender was entrusted with its execution, while Bach retained the supervision. He had, of course, long left the town before work on the instrument was completed, but he was able to come as a guest and play it at the service of dedication. This organ was in use at the St Blasiuskirche until 1821 when it was replaced by a new one of no importance. However, in 1959 Bach's project of 1708 was realized for a second time and Mühlhausen is unique in possessing the only new example of an authentic Bach organ.

Some of the reasons for his early departure from Mühlhausen were cautiously indicated in his letter of resignation written on June 25, 1708. It was evident that in spite of his simple way of living he could 'exist only in strained circumstances', taking into account the modest fees he demanded at first, and that, in the meantime, he had married. The deciding factor, however, was that he found it impossible to realize his 'final aim, namely the establishment of a proper church music to the glory of God in the face of adversities, and that there was no hope that this might come about one day, as it should do, to the edification of the very soul of this church.'

We know that these 'adversities' were caused by the fanatical struggle between the Orthodox Church and the Pietists. Mühlhausen had become once again,

Since 1959 the Blasiuskirche of Mühlhausen has once more possessed a 'Bach organ'. It was reconstructed after the composer's design, which has been preserved

as in 1525, the time of Thomas Münzer, the central battlefield of ecclesiastical disputes. We may assume that Bach's very real devotion, unhindered by dogmatic limitations, eschewed theological squabbles; however, the practical effects of this quarrel must have forced him to take sides. A man who, like the pietistic superintendent Johann Adolf Frohne, tried to hinder the development of concerted church music could only be Bach's enemy, while the orthodox vicar Georg Christian Eilmar became his friend by offering him free scope for his muse. It was most unfortunate, therefore, that Bach's immediate superior at the St Blasiuskirche should be the Pietist, and that the orthodox vicar of the Marienkirche could be of no official assistance to him.

Bach had to face the situation resulting from these unfortunate circumstances which even the council, though well disposed towards him, could not alter. He submitted a well-written and diplomatic letter of resignation and this was acknowledged in the council meeting of June 26, 1708 with the remark:

The pietistic superintendent Frohne (far left), and
the orthodox parson Eilmar – both involved in
theological disputes affecting Bach's stay in Mühlhausen

On June 25, 1708 Johann Sebastian asked the Mühlhausen council if he could be
relieved from his post as organist

In 1708 Bach moved to Weimar. His new employer was a prince,
Duke Wilhelm Ernst of Sachsen-Weimar (right)

'Since it was impossible to prevent his leaving, the resignation should be
accepted.' With the express request that he oblige the city by continuing to
supervise the organ construction, the engagement was terminated on a concilia-
tory note, and when a new composition was needed the following February,
again for the inauguration of the new council, Bach was happy to write the
work and direct the performance. Unfortunately this particular *Ratswechsel-
kantate* has not been found to this day, although, like the earlier composition,
it had appeared in print.

Bach in Weimar   It would have been against Bach's nature to leave with an uncertain future
before him. His prospective field of activity had been known to him for some
time. During a visit to Weimar he played at the ducal court and had received

Der Durchlauchtigste Fürst und Herr, Herr Wilhelm Ernst, Hertzog zu Sachßen,
Julich, Cleve und Bergen auch Engern und Westphalen, Landgraf in Thuringen Marckgraf zu
Meißen gefürsteter Graf zu Henneberg, Graf zu der Marck und Ravensberg, Herr zu Ravens.

Der hohen Sachßen zier der Schmuck Durchlauchter welt
Wird hier von kunstlers hand im Schatten vorgestellt
Doch sieht man Gottes bild auß seiner Seele strahlen,
und seinen Himmels geist sich selbst durchs Leben mahlen.

Pet: Schenck fec: et exc: Amstel.   S.F.S.   cum Privilegio

31

The old Stadtkirche in Weimar

In 1732 the organist of the Stadtkirche
in Weimar, Johann Sebastian's cousin Walther,
published his *Musicalisches Lexicon*,
mentioning for the first time
biographical information concerning the composer

'the gracious invitation from His Highness the Duke of Sachsen-Weimar to join the court orchestra and chamber music'. Bach felt highly honoured, and regarded this proposition as a fortunate turn of events since it promised to bring him a good deal nearer his 'final aim . . . of achieving a properly established church music'.

The move was, in fact a return to familiar surroundings. Bach's former employer, Duke Johann Ernst, had died, but the prospect of renewing friendly relations with two music-loving princes meant a great deal to him. Besides, his new position as a member of the chamber music ensemble and as organist to the court offered far more scope than there had been five years earlier. The reigning duke, Wilhelm Ernst, was a man with high moral standards, well disposed towards the arts and sciences, who did much to prepare the ground for the golden age of Goethe's time.

Weimar then had only 5,000 inhabitants, yet Bach found a great number of

A church concert,
the frontispiece
of Walther's
Musicalisches Lexicon

cultured persons in this small place. His horizon, both as man and artist, was enlarged, and to us to-day these nine years in Weimar appear as a period of turbulent development from which was to emerge a mature personality.

Bach was happy to work in the vicinity of his second cousin Johann Gottfried Walther, the organist at the Stadtkirche. A real friendship of artists developed between these two men of equal age and similar ideas, and led them to a free exchange of their experiences on composition. In his *Musicalisches Lexicon* of 1732 Walther was the first to publish biographical data of his 'cousin and godfather' which end with this remark: 'The family of Bach is said to have originally come from Hungary and all who bear this name were, as far as one can tell, dedicated to the cause of music, perhaps because even the letters B A C H in this order constitute a melody.* (This idea was first expressed by Mr Bach of Leipzig.)'

Johann Sebastian was successful in his search for friends. One of them, Salomo Franck, was an honoured personality of the court with the titles of Secretary to the Council, Court Librarian and Administrator to the Mint Cabinet. Bach favoured his profound and sincere texts when composing his cantatas. Christoph Kiesewetter, Bach's former headmaster at Ohrdruf, was transferred to Weimar in 1712. Three years later he was joined by the eminent philologist and scholar Johann Matthias Gesner, who expressed his admiration for the composer's

*In German musical notation B = B flat and H = B natural. (Transl.)

The 'Wilhelmsburg' palace in Weimar where Bach performed his works

Prince Ernst August of Sachsen-Weimar

genius with great eloquence. The two men met again later, when Gesner was rector at St Thomas's in Leipzig.

From the economic angle, too, Weimar represented an improvement. His salary here, of 158 florins, was well in excess of what he had received in Mühlhausen, and his income rose gradually to twice this amount with the growing appreciation of his achievements. Holding the title of 'Kammermusicus', Bach automatically became a member of the court orchestra comprising, as a rule, fourteen chamber-musicians, seven trumpeters and one tympanist. Their names and functions, entered carefully over a period of years in the 'register of court officials', have been preserved. As was the custom at all the smaller courts, the establishment of an orchestra was guaranteed by the employment of the musicians in a secondary capacity, such as secretary, page, butler, etc. The orchestral

Corelli, one of the Italian
composers who greatly influenced
the new concert style
of the early 18th century

duties consisted of playing in the church services at the Schlosskirche, taking part
in concerts of chamber music in the ducal apartments of the 'Wilhelmsburg',
making music while meals were partaken, at serenades or masquerades in the
ducal gardens, at festive open-air performances and official memorial services.
Perhaps Bach was one of the 'sixteen well trained musicians' who had to play
occasionally in heyduck costumes for the amusement of the Duke and his
friends.

   Johann Sebastian's function in the chamber music ensemble was probably
mainly that of a violinist but occasionally he may have played the cembalo as
well, and we may assume that he composed or arranged some occasional music.
In 1714 he became *Konzertmeister*, second only in rank to the deputy *Kapell-*

Antonio Vivaldi – his violin
concertos were very important
to the musical life
at Weimar in Bach's time

meister whose duties he gradually took over. The old and frail *Kapellmeister*,
Johann Samuel Drese, and his moderately talented son and deputy Johann
Wilhelm Drese contributed little towards the development of the chamber
orchestra.

A chamber ensemble with a style of its own played at the 'Rote Schloss' in
the vicinity of the 'Wilhelmsburg'. Here lived the widow of the former Duke,
Johann Ernst, and her two music-loving sons, the Princes Ernst August and
Johann Ernst. Bach's cousin, Johann Georg Walther was also a frequent visitor
as the Princes' tutor in this establishment, where a special interest was shown in
music in the modern Italian style, which was then causing a stir all over Europe.
Inspired by the violin concertos of the great Venetian composer Vivaldi,

In the Schlosskirche Bach performed his cantatas written for the
church services of the court. He ordered the organ (on the highest gallery)
to be thoroughly renovated. This was completed in 1714

Johann Ernst, the younger and more talented of the two Princes, himself composed a number of interesting concertos, while Walther and Bach transcribed
some Italian and some German concertos for keyboard instruments. Bach must
have made good use of this opportunity to master the new Italian 'concerto
manner' which, by introducing a lively interchange between concertante solo
parts and orchestral tutti passages, created new harmonies and contrasts. The
style of his later violin and keyboard concertos, including the *Italian Concerto*
for solo piano, benefited from this experience.

As organist to the court, Johann Sebastian was appointed successor to
Johann Effler, a musician of some standing. Nothing is mentioned in the Weimar
records about the organ except that it was new and came from the workshop
of Johann Conrad Weishaupt of Seebergen near Gotha. In matters concerning
the organ, Bach's demands were always most exacting and this is illustrated by
the fact that only a few years later he declared that the instrument was inadequate and that it should therefore be rebuilt. It is significant that, exactly as in
Mühlhausen, his first demand was for the addition of a carillon, whereupon
one was purchased at the Leipzig fair from a merchant of Nuremberg. A little
later, the master organ-builder Trebs was commissioned to undertake a radical
reconstruction for which Bach presumably made the plans. The work on the
organ, finished at great expense in 1714, was tangible proof of the high regard
in which Bach was held as organist and expert after so short a time at the court.

During these years he must have been bewitched by the organ. He composed
an abundance of toccatas, fantasias, preludes and fugues, and his genius was
as much in evidence as his virtuosity and inventiveness. These works constitute
the essence of a development which made him into the greatest of German
organists, and his fame as such was spreading rapidly.

Constantin Bellermann, rector at Münden, later gave us his vivid impressions in these words: 'His feet seemed to fly across the pedals as if they were
winged, and mighty sounds filled the church.' And the 'Nekrolog' related:
'His fingers were all of equal strength, all equally able to play with the finest
precision. He had invented so comfortable a fingering that he could master the
most difficult parts with perfect ease . . . He was able to accomplish passages

on the pedals with his feet which would have given trouble to the five fingers of many a clever player on the keyboard.'

Organ pupils came from everywhere and various towns approached him with requests to test or dedicate a new organ. Philipp Emanuel has given his own account of what generally happened on those occasions:

'Never before had organs been tested so critically and thoroughly. He knew everything about organ-building . . . he understood the use of the stops better than anyone. It often happened that organists began to fear for their organs when he proceeded to pull out stops which in their opinion would never be able to produce a good sound; but when they heard the result, they were amazed. At the beginning of a test he used to say for fun: "Above all I must know whether this organ has a good lung," and, pulling out the stops he produced the biggest sound possible. This often made the organ-builders go pale with fright.'

Bach had become so well known that in 1713 he was offered the post of organist at the Liebfrauenkirche in Halle, previously held until his death by Handel's teacher Friedrich Wilhelm Zachau. The offer was made after the performance of a trial cantata. Bach was particularly tempted by the big organ under construction there, but neither the conditions laid down in the contract nor the salary came up to his expectations, so that he put in for a better offer

Halle in the 18th century. Right: Aria from the cantata *Bereitet die Wege* in Bach's handwriting

41

since no one could expect him to 'change his employment and not improve it'.

The board at Halle was annoyed. However, where money matters were concerned Bach was by no means unrealistic; besides, he had to care for a growing family. The first child Catherina Dorothea was born in December 1708, Wilhelm Friedemann in November 1710, twins were born in February 1713 but died soon after birth, Carl Philipp Emanuel was born in March 1714 and finally Johann Gottfried Bernhard in May 1715.

Bach as
Konzertmeister

The composer's promotion to the rank of *Konzertmeister* in the spring of 1714 has already been mentioned. Apart from his normal duties he had to 'perform new pieces each month'. This meant the composition of a new cantata every four weeks for the service in the Schlosskirche, a condition likewise imposed on his predecessors. For three years Bach supplied the appropriate works, thus approaching his ideal of a 'properly established church music'. The best texts for these compositions were provided by Salomo Franck's collections of poems, the most rewarding of which bore the informative title 'Evangelisches Andachts-Opffer (Evangelic Offering of Devotion), to His Highness the Duke and Ruler . . . in spiritual cantatas to be performed on Sundays and Holy Occasions in the Court Chapel of the Wilhelmsburg in the year 1715, inspired by Salomo Franck, Chief Secretary to the Council of the whole Duchy of Sachsen-Weimar'.

The new church
music

During this particular period the form of the cantata underwent a considerable change. Until then the text for such a work was taken from the Bible or a sacred song, and composed in the manner of the German church concert, that is to say, with a free interchange of arias and choral episodes. Now, however, new forms of expression came into church music from the fashionable Italian operas. A pioneer in the field of texts for church cantatas was the parson Erdmann Neumeister, born near Weissenfels, but later to work in Hamburg, who himself related how he came to write poetry: 'When the normal Sunday duties were done, I endeavoured for my own edification to cast into poetic form the foremost ideas of the sermon, and thus to revive the mind, tired from preaching, with agreeable thoughts from which . . . the present cantatas originated.' He confessed that they really looked 'like a piece from an opera made up of recitatives and arias', and these texts were gladly taken up by certain progressive composers, among them Georg Philipp Telemann.

Bach too used some of them, but eventually he found his ideal partner in Salomo Franck. The now familiar Christmas Cantata *Tritt auf die Glaubensbahn* is one well-known instance of their collaboration, and because of the colourful use of recorders and violas it is one of the most charming creations in this field. It is vastly different from the *Actus Tragicus*, written only a few

Duke Christian of Sachsen-Weissenfels. The *Jagdkantate* was performed for his birthday in Febuary 1716

Erdmann Neumeister – by introducing operatic elements into his texts he brought new life into church music

43

years before and based on similar tonal colouring but, in accordance with the old ideas of form, more closely connected with Biblical compositions.

Almost the entire output of the Weimar cantatas was kept within the limits of the lyrical chamber music style, appropriate to the rather small dimensions of the Schlosskapelle. Where the sound texture was richer and the scope broader, the work must have been written for a special occasion, such as, for instance, the cantata in eleven movements *Ich hatte viel Bekümmernis*, in which the trumpets are used rather prominently. This work was intended as a farewell to Prince Johann Ernst, who left Weimar in July 1714 for the Taunus, in a last attempt to find a cure for his serious illness. It was in vain: he died a year later in Frankfurt at the early age of nineteen. It would be hard to find a more exalted movement in the whole of Bach's works than the powerful final fugue on the words from the book of Revelations '*Lob und Ehre und Preis und Gewalt sei unserm Gott von Ewigkeit zu Ewigkeit*'. ('Blessing and honour and glory and power be unto our God for ever and ever.')

The obvious duties of an official poet included the glorification of birthdays and marriages, state visits, celebrations and memorial services. In Franck's collected poems we find, therefore, a number of secular works written for special occasions in cantata form, and we know that Bach, as leader of the orchestra, was one of the composers who wrote music to these texts. Unfortunately only one of these compositions has been preserved, the rest are either lost or perhaps used as material in other works. When in February 1716 Wilhelm Ernst paid a

visit to his friend the Duke Christian of Weissenfels, the crowning event was the performance of an unusual composition. The orchestra had come from Weimar to perform the *Jagdkantate* written by Franck and Bach, in which mythological figures sang in praise of the host. Evidently Bach was very fond of this entertaining cantata, consisting of six recitatives, seven arias and two choral movements, since he used it again later on several occasions. He also took three pieces from the work, enlarged them and changed the words before they were incorporated into church cantatas. A Whitsun cantata, for instance, contains the aria *Mein gläubiges Herze, frohlocke, sing, scherze*, which originated from the pastoral aria of the Weissenfels hunting music, '*Weil die wollenreichen Herden*'.

In 1717 Bach met the famous keyboard virtuoso Louis Marchand. There are many legends about this meeting and countless versions exist describing Bach's 'bloodless' victory over his rival; the one cited in the 'Nekrolog' is perhaps the most authentic: 'The famous French virtuoso Marchand had come to Dresden and so pleased the king with his performance that he was offered employment at the royal court and promised a very good salary. The Dresden *Konzertmeister* of the day, Volumier, wrote to Bach, whose merits were not unknown to him, and told him to come to Dresden without delay and to challenge the arrogant Marchand to a musical contest. Bach gladly accepted the invitation and travelled to Dresden where Volumier received him with pleasure and arranged for him to listen to Marchand without being seen. Bach sent a polite note to Marchand saying

Part of the autograph of the Weissenfels *Jagdkantate*

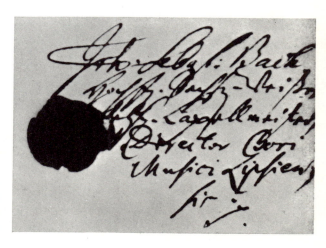

Bach's signature as Kapellmeister to the court of Sachsen-Weissenfels (1731). In all probability the birthday cantata of 1716 subsequently led to this nomination

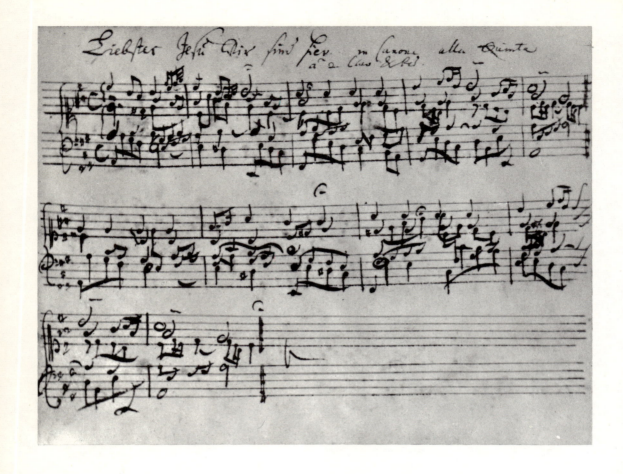

that he was prepared to extemporize on any music Marchand would care to set him, and that he expected the same from him, thus challenging him to a musical competition. Such audacity! Marchand readily accepted. Day and place were determined, not without the knowledge of the king, and Bach appeared at the appointed hour on a battlefield for which the house of a distinguished minister had been chosen. A company of high-ranking persons of both sexes were assembled there, but Marchand kept them waiting for a long time. Finally, the host sent to Marchand's quarters reminding him, in case he had forgotten, that the time had now come to prove himself. To everyone's amazement, however, it transpired that Monsieur Marchand had left Dresden that very morning

A page of the *Orgelbüchlein*, a collection
of choral preludes, perhaps written
while Bach was under arrest in Weimar

The famous French organist Louis Marchand
accepted Bach's invitation to a
musical contest, but failed to appear

LOUIS MARCHAND
Organiste du Roy
Né à Lion, Mort à Paris le 17 Février
1732. Âgé de 61 ans

by the fastest coach. Bach, who had carried the day without a fight, now had
occasion to show how well armed he had been against his opponent. This he
did, and all present were astounded. The king ordered a present of 500 thalers
to be given to the composer, but a certain dishonest servant, who thought that
he could make better use of this present, appropriated the sum, and thus Bach
brought home as only reward for his efforts the honour of the victory.'

Johann Sebastian's success did not prevent him from running into private
and professional difficulties during his stay in Weimar. Having left the intricate
theological quarrels behind him at Mühlhausen, he was now drawn into court
intrigues of growing intensity. The conflicts between the households of the

'Wilhelmsburg' and the 'Rote Schloss' were unending owing to an old dispute over the inheritance. By tradition the court musicians were servants common to both establishments, but eventually the jealous Wilhelm Ernst strictly forbade any music-making in the house of his nephew Ernst August. Since Bach was in every way on excellent terms with the inhabitants of the 'Rote Schloss' he could hardly obey this rule, and so inevitably aroused the Duke's annoyance. The conditions became unbearable for Bach when the Duke appointed Drese's mediocre son to succeed his father, who had died, as *Kapellmeister*, thus by-passing the man who had for some time past been virtually directing the music at court as leader of the orchestra.

The Duke's decision was more reasonable than it appears since the Drese family had been of service to the court for a long time, and the young *Kapell-meister* had studied in Italy. All the same this was a bitter disappointment for

In 1717 Bach became *Kapellmeister* and director of chamber music at the castle of Köthen. His portrait was painted by Ihle about three years later (right)

Prince Leopold of Anhalt-Köthen,
Johann Sebastian's new master

Title page of
a serenade for Prince
Leopold's birthday

Bach. He reduced the work he did in the course of his duties to the barest mini-
mum and began to look for a new position elsewhere. In this he may have had
the help of Duke Ernst August, who introduced Bach to the court of Prince
Leopold, the brother of Ernst August's wife, at Köthen. This resulted in
an invitation to Bach to become *Kapellmeister* of the court orchestra there,
but a polite request to be relieved of his post in Weimar was rejected outright
by Duke Wilhelm Ernst. It seems likely that Bach then made preparations to
leave Weimar secretly, whereupon the Duke, his pride offended, decided to
take firm action. The court secretary, Bormann, has left us the following account:

'On the 6th of November the orchestral leader and court organist Bach was
arrested by reason of a stubborn attempt to obtain his dismissal by force. He
was finally released and dismissed on the 2nd of December, the Duke's dis-
pleasure having been brought to his notice by the court secretary.'

*Bach under
arrest*

What an unpleasant final discord! Yet, it may be that Bach composed during
these four weeks of enforced solitude that unique annual cycle of choral preludes
the *Orgelbüchlein*, which Albert Schweitzer called 'the dictionary of Bach's
language in sound'. 'To the glory of God alone in the highest, to further
the learning of one and all' is the motto written on the title page of this inexhaustible 'dictionary'.

Now Bach, at the age of thirty-two, held the highest position the Baroque age could offer a musician, and as *Kapellmeister* of the court orchestra he made his entry into the small capital of Anhalt-Köthen. The contemporary musicologist Johann Mattheson defined this much coveted office, which had long since taken precedence over that of civic precentor in the musical hierarchy, in the following terms: 'The *Capellmeister of Köthen* is a learned court official and a composer of the highest order. He is responsible for directing, arranging and composing sacred as well as secular music at the court of an emperor, king or duke, and for the supervision of the performances: to the glory of God, the pleasure of his master, and for the benefit of the entire court. Sometimes he has between fifty and a hundred persons under his command'.

So grand an establishment was well beyond the means of the miniature court of Anhalt-Köthen. The young prince stretched his budget to the limit when he increased the orchestra to eighteen players. The musicians who formed this capable ensemble were all good artists, and some of them had been engaged from Berlin. Besides, the orchestra compared favourably with many another, as the members had been chosen on purely musical grounds, and not, as was customary, to make a showpiece of the band.

The young and friendly Leopold was an exception among the princes of Bach's time, in that he had acquired a considerable proficiency with the violin, the viola da gamba, and the cembalo. He had received some voice training and had studied theory with the famous composer Johann David Heinichen. On his many travels he had become acquainted with the music that was currently being written for concert and opera, and brushing aside court etiquette, he made music freely with his court musicians. Thus he created an atmosphere of equality, devoid of all prejudice, on both the personal and the artistic level. He was particularly well disposed towards his director of music and had the highest regard for him.

As a token of this sincere friendship the Prince, his younger brother Augustus, and their sister Eleonore Wilhelmine, became godparents to Bach's seventh child. It was named Leopold Augustus and baptised on November 17, 1718. In these surroundings where he was appreciated as a person and as an artist, where his rank, both socially and financially, was equal to that of a court chamberlain, Bach felt more at ease than ever before. It is understandable therefore that he hoped things might continue this way, since here in Köthen he was able to

One of the solo sonatas for
violin, composed in Köthen,
which demand great virtuosity
from the player

live happily and compose freely. He later expressed this in a letter to his friend and
former schoolmate Erdmann: 'There I had a gracious prince as master, who knew
music as well as he loved it, and I had hoped to remain in his service until the end
of my life.' These words, sincere without doubt, show how different Bach's music
would have been if his wish never to leave Köthen had come true. A golden age
of German instrumental music might have resulted, and the whole course of
musical history been changed. Bach's output of instrumental works during these
six years was phenomenal.

The compositions for official use at court were written expressly for the court
orchestra. The records of the Anhalt archives give a clear picture of the men
employed under Bach, and of their musical abilities. The names of the trumpeters, the woodwind, the principal and rank-and-file string-players are all
known. For special occasions the orchestra was augmented by musicians — say,

In 1721 Bach dedicated six compositions to the Margrave Christian Ludwig of Brandenburg. These were the *Brandenburg Concertos*

Christianus Ludovicus, Marggraf zu Brandenburg.

two horn players — from elsewhere. These, then, were the chosen artists, whose privilege it was to assist at the first performances of Bach's new works.

The melodious sonatas for violin, flute or viola da gamba were more in harmony with Prince Leopold's candle-lit music room; on these occasions the composer presumably played the cembalo part. The solo sonatas for violin or violoncello demand an almost superhuman technique. The basically melodic instrument has to play harmonic and even polyphonic figures in these works, as for instance in the fugal movements or even in that miracle of a piece, the *Chaconne*. No mightier music than the variations in this work has ever been written for the four strings of a single instrument.

Intended for a bigger circle of players and listeners were the concertos for solo instruments with orchestral accompaniment, among them the violin concertos: one, in A minor, severe and masculine, the other, a happy work in E

The beginning of the first movement of the sixth

Brandenburg Concerto in B flat major in full score

major; or the moving double concerto in D minor with a melodious duet in the largo movement.

With the *concerts avec plusieurs instruments* Bach surprised his musicians by introducing new sound combinations. Every one of these works has a character of its own, as the group of soloists is different in each case.

In the spring 1721 Bach chose six such concertos, copied them beautifully into a magnificent oblong volume, added a dedication written in French and sent the whole to the Margrave Christian Ludwig of Brandenburg who had commissioned the composer to write these works for his orchestra. Hence the name *Brandenburg Concertos*. They are, however, written to suit the conditions at Köthen. Not only did he take into consideration the instruments he had available, but he paid particular attention to the abilities of his musicians. The trumpeter who could master the last movement of the second concerto must have been capable of an astounding virtuosity. While Bach probably played the cembalo part in the fifth concerto, Prince Leopold presumably took part in the sixth of the series, so remarkable for its sombre viola and viola da gamba tone.

With great enthusiasm, Bach dedicated himself to the composition of works for the keyboard: Fantasies, Toccatas, Preludes and Fugues followed one another in quick succession. Some of them, as perhaps the *Chromatic Fantasy and Fugue*, may have delighted the audience at court, but on the whole these pieces were destined for the calmer conditions of music-making at home. Apart from music for the 'heart's delight', he wrote an increasing number of educational pieces. Wilhelm Friedemann was now nine years of age, old enough therefore to join in with his father's pupils and to be given proper schooling. On January 22, 1720 his father carefully made for him the *Clavierbüchlein vor Wilhelm Friedemann Bach*, a book of instructions and exercises intended for very swift but thorough progress. Nothing was left out: neither an explanation of the old clefs and notes, nor the rules of ornamentation and the principle of fingering. The sixty-two pieces, mostly original and of various lengths, are on the whole anything but easy for beginners.

In the later collections of Bach's compositions, many of them appear again in a more extended and mature form: a case in point is the double volume of two- and three-part *inventions*. These tuneful and polyphonic pieces, developed from tiny motifs, began a new era of German keyboard music, and constitute to this day the musical Bible of every aspiring pianist. It is clearly stated in the preface that this 'collection of studies' was intended to further a thorough musical education by teaching clean execution of polyphonic passages, by

To facilitate the musical education of his sons, Bach devised his own instruction books.
The *Clavierbüchlein vor Wilhelm Friedemann Bach*, begun in 1720, is an example

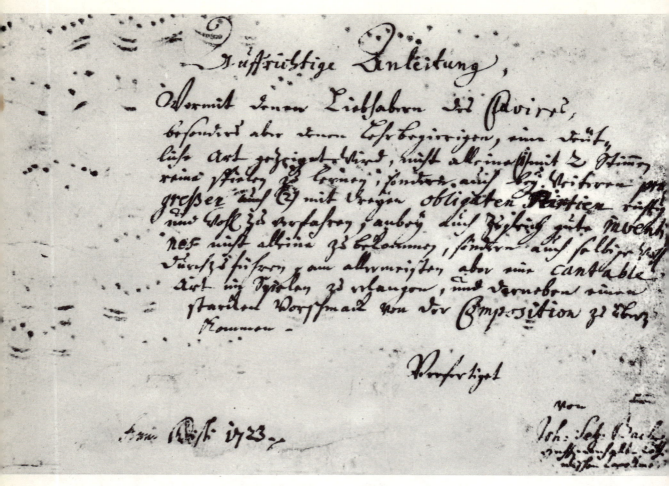

Title page of the two- and three-part inventions. No. 14 of the two-part inventions (right).

encouraging the invention and development of musical motifs, by teaching people to play with a singing tone, and finally by giving them an insight into the technique of composition.

If the *inventions* still adhered to the common keys of Baroque music, Bach broke completely new ground with another composite work. The theoretical basis for this innovation was the treatise '*Die musikalische Temperatur*', written by the Halberstadt organist Andreas Werkmeister in 1691. In this work he declared the current system of tuning to be inadequate, since it necessarily limited the use of tonalities. He advocated a system of 'even-tempered tuning'

These pieces were the beginning of a new epoch in keyboard music

which, although altering the pure intervals slightly, allowed a complete freedom of harmony and modulation on the keyboard. Some composers had already begun to explore the new field. Johann Kaspar Ferdinand Fischer is one of them, and his 'Ariadne musica', a work of twenty short preludes and fugues, is an example. But Bach was the first to cover all the ground when he composed his twenty-four preludes and fugues in 1722 'in all tones and semitones'. He called this work the *Wohltemperirte Clavier*. The abundance of ideas it contains profoundly impressed his pupils and still influences musicians, including the contemporaries Hindemith and Shostakovitch.

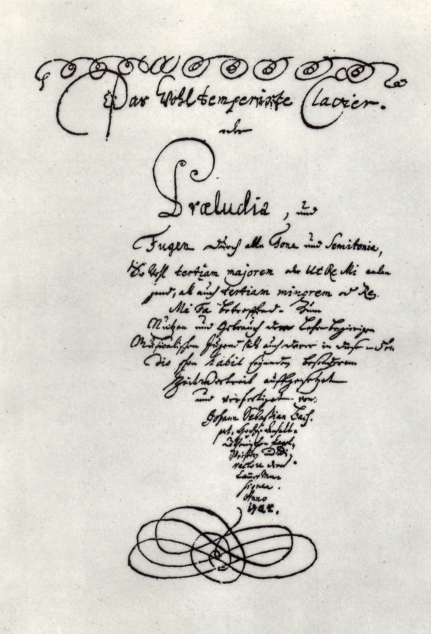

The decorative title page of the *Wohltemperirte Clavier* (1722)

Beginning of the E major fugue from the *Wohltemperirte Clavier*

Bach went twice with Prince Leopold to Karlsbad

For his family and pupils Bach wrote the charming *French Suites*. The gentle clavichord was perhaps most suited for these graceful dance movements, while it seems likely that the bigger and more difficult *English Suites* were intended for the cembalo, particularly because of the ambitious preludes.

Bach's days, at court and at home, were completely taken up with music. Since the Prince was loth to miss his musical entertainment even when travelling, some members of his court orchestra accompanied him whenever possible. Thus, with his cembalo and several musicians of the chamber ensemble, Bach went twice to Karlsbad, the meeting place of the European aristocracy, where the Prince was spending his holiday.

After his wife's death Johann Sebastian looked for a new post in Hamburg

The Schnitger organ of the Jacobikirche in Hamburg

When he returned from the second journey in July 1720, he had the worst shock of his life: his wife had died. The 'Nekrolog' gave this account of the sad event:

'He had been happily married for thirteen years to his first wife when, in 1720, on his return to Köthen from a journey with his Prince to Karlsbad, he learned to his great sorrow that his wife was dead and buried. He had left her a

Death of
Maria Barbara

strong and healthy woman, and not before he had crossed his threshold, did he hear that she had died as the result of an illness'.

The wish to leave this place of painful memory was probably Bach's first reaction. Two months later found him already interested in the post of organist at the Jacobikirche in Hamburg, which had been held until his death by Heinrich Friese. Bach must have been tempted by the wonderful Schnitger organ with four manuals and sixty stops, which is today one of the world's most precious historical instruments. However, he left Hamburg for Köthen before the audition, presumably because the conditions there did not suit him. But the journey had not been in vain. Bach had played Variations on the Chorale 'By the waters

In 1725 Bach began another notebook
for his wife Anna Magdalena; it
gradually grew into a richly filled
music book. The illustration shows a song
in Anna Magdalena's hand

of Babylon' on the organ of the Katherinenkirche to the old Dutch organist
Jan Adams Reinken, whose words of appreciation confirmed Bach's mastery.
Perhaps on this occasion he also played the *G-minor Fugue*, which is based on
a Dutch folksong.

At Köthen Bach only wrote a few occasional organ compositions; the reformed
church at court made no demands on him in this respect. Furthermore, there
was no place for a cantata in the Divine Service of the Calvinists. The young
Prince, however, was by no means narrow-minded, and at the beginning of his
reign he issued a proclamation of tolerance. The Church of Köthen was therefore rather more tolerant of Protestant music than was customary elsewhere,
and at least on festive occasions Bach could make music to his heart's content.

The court accounts are the sole source of information about Bach's numerous
cantata compositions for New Year or the Prince's birthday, two occasions
which were always celebrated by the performance of two cantatas, one sacred
and one secular. Although no permanent choir was available, Bach could
always count on singers who were under contract to the court. One of them, a
certain Anna Magdalena Wilke, daughter of a court trumpeter, first at Zeitz,
later at Weissenfels, is mentioned as 'singer to the court' from 1721 onwards,
but it is not known when Bach first noticed her 'rather fine soprano voice'. At
all events, the purely artistic interest gradually grew into a more personal
relationship. On December 3, 1721, the wedding took place in Bach's house,
with the express approval of the Prince. Anna Magdalena continued to draw
her considerable salary after Bach's second marriage, a most welcome addition
to Bach's income. In the course of twenty-eight happy years, thirteen children
were born to Anna Magdalena Bach, who was sixteen years younger than her
husband. Apart from all her work in the house, she found time to continue
with her singing and to help the composer in his work. Numerous scores and parts
were copied beautifully by her hand, and in the course of time her writing
became so similar to that of her husband that it is often difficult to tell them apart;
but unfortunately, we do not know what she looked like. She must have been
portrayed in a painting belonging to Philipp Emanuel, but this disappeared

*Bach's second
marriage*

67

soon after his death. Her character is described in very warm terms by Johann
Elias Bach, a cousin of the composer, in a letter written at a later date. She
loved song-birds and flowers, he wrote, and 'like a child, she would look forward
to receive some such gift at Christmas' and she would 'care for it as for a little
child, so that it might not die'.

The two music books Bach prepared in 1722 and 1725 for his young wife and
helper in all musical matters bear witness to this happy marriage: the first, a
small and simple oblong volume, contained five *French Suites* and several smaller pieces; the second, a precious book in green and gold with the initials A.M.B.
and the year 1725 stamped on the cover, became a kind of musical family album,
into which Bach, his wife, and his growing children entered a miscellaneous
collection of pieces and songs, gay and serious, entertaining and instructive,
some original and some copied compositions, and even a short instruction on
the figured bass. *Erbauliche Gedanken eines Tabaksrauchers*, the chorale *Dir,
Dir, Jehova*, the arias *Willst Du Dein Herz mir schenken* and *Bist Du bei mir*,
give an idea of the variety of subjects.

Bach's quiet wedding was followed only a few days later by the pageantry
marking the Prince's marriage to the Princess Friederika Henrietta of Anhalt-
Bernburg. When Bach composed an ode of homage for this wedding he did
not realize that he had come to the turning-point of his career.

The handwriting of Bach's second wife Anna Magdalena

FRIEDERICA HENRIETTA.

*Gebohrne und vermählte Fürstin
zu Anhalt, Hertzogin zu Sachsen,
Engern und Westphalen, Graeffin
zu Ascanien Frau zu Berenburg
und Zerbst.*

In 1722 Bach applied for the post of cantor at St Thomas's in Leipzig

The new princess, whose smooth and doll-like face is pictured on a contemporary portrait, was not in favour of her husband's musical activities. She managed, by exerting constant pressure, 'to make the musical inclination of the said Prince somewhat luke-warm', as Bach wrote later in a letter. His vital interests threatened, he once more began to look for a position elsewhere, and, keeping the education of his sons in mind, now turned to a university town.

But the friendly relations with Prince Leopold were evidently not affected, as the certificate of dismissal was couched in the most amicable terms. Later, when his first keyboard partita was printed in Leipzig, Bach dedicated it to the new-born Crown Prince; finally he wrote the funeral music for the death of Leopold, which, though the Prince died in November 1728, was not given its first performance until March 1729.

Bach's predecessor at St Thomas's: Johann Kuhnau

In Leipzig the post of cantor at St Thomas's School had been vacant since the death of Johann Kuhnau on June 5, 1722. A long line of eminent church musicians had held this post in the past. Kuhnau, a versatile artist and an excellent scholar, had worked at the Thomaskirche for thirty-eight years, first as organist, later as cantor. He had done his best to raise the general standard of church music, and had fervently opposed the influence of opera on school music.

The council of Leipzig was obviously trying to fill the vacancy with a musician of some standing. The first choice was therefore Georg Philipp Telemann, director of music at Hamburg, whose name carried a lot of weight in Leipzig. The older inhabitants remembered him as a talented law student, who had made his name as director of a *collegium musicum* formed by students, as organist at the Neukirche, and even as a composer of operas. By that time he had already

Georg Philipp Telemann
was elected successor
to Kuhnau, but did
not go to Leipzig

Graupner was the next to
be elected, but had to
decline. The way was
now free for Bach

been given to understand by the council that should the ailing Kuhnau die prematurely, he would be considered for the cantorship of St Thomas's.

The city fathers were therefore highly gratified when they saw his name twenty years later among the six applicants for the post of cantor left vacant by the death of Kuhnau. The council lost no time in inviting the famous composer to come to Leipzig on August 9 and 10 for the obligatory cantata audition.

All his conditions were gladly accepted and he was at once elected, the result being formally announced in the council chambers on August 13. Provided with a considerable sum for travelling expenses, Telemann returned to Hamburg where, good business man that he was, he succeeded in getting his salary increased. Only after many weeks did he send a definite refusal to the impatiently-waiting council in Leipzig.

These developments gave rise to a general feeling of disappointment and annoyance; nevertheless an eligible musician had to be found among the remaining applicants. In the minutes of the council meeting on December 21, two names were mentioned for the first time, both of importance for the final decision, 'Capellmeister Graupner in Darmstadt und Bach in Köthen'. Of these two, Christoph Graupner, a pupil of Kuhnau familiar from his student

Revers des Cantoris bey der Thomas=
Schule H: Johann Sebastian Bachen.

Demnach bey E. E. Hochw. Rathe der Stadt
Leipzig ich meiner benanter zu dem bey der
Thomas=Schule daselbst vacanten Cantor
Dienste mich gewaldet, und desfalls ich
meine Person zu respectiren geziemend ge=
beten, Soll verspreche ich Kraft die=
ses, daß dafern meine Suche statt finden
und mir solcher Dienst auffgetragen werden
solte, ich nicht nur binnen dato und
zu der frühestens drey Wochen
von der bey dem Durchlaucht. Anhalt=
Cöthischen Hofe aus mir habenden Bestallung
mich los machen und derselbe Vorzeigung
dem Rathe der dimission=Schein auffzu=
zeigen, sondern auch, wenn ich solchen Can=
tor=Dienst würcklich antrete, mich aber
Schul=Ordnung, so bereits vorhanden, oder
noch auffgerichtet werden müste, mich gemäß
verhalten, absonderlich aber die Knaben,
so auff die Schule recipiret werden, nicht
alleine in denen darzu gehörigen ordent=
lichen Stunden, sondern auch privatissime
im Singen ohne Entgelt informiren, und
Was mir sonst darbey zu thun obliegt, mit
allenthalben gebührend verrichten, nicht

Bach had to assure the Leipzig council of his goodwill and certify his readiness
to do his duty according to the rules even before his election

days with the conditions at Leipzig, seemed the best choice. On the occasion of
a visit to his relatives at Christmas 1722 he had played in various churches in
Leipzig, and on January 17, he passed his official cantata audition with distinction. In a respectful letter to the Prince of Hesse the council asked that
Graupner be released from his services. The answer was not only a definite
refusal, but the Prince, by raising Graupner's salary, succeeded in binding him
closer to the court of Darmstadt. The city fathers regarded this further check
to their efforts as a great misfortune. The mayor and councillor to the court of
appeal, Platz, only expressed the general opinion when he spoke these
memorable words at the meeting on April 9, which secured him a mention
in Bach's biography: 'Since the best cannot be had, one must take the next best.'
  Bach, one of these 'next best', submitted the cantata *Jesus nahm zu sich die
Zwölfe*, for his audition on February 7. A Hamburg newspaper reported that

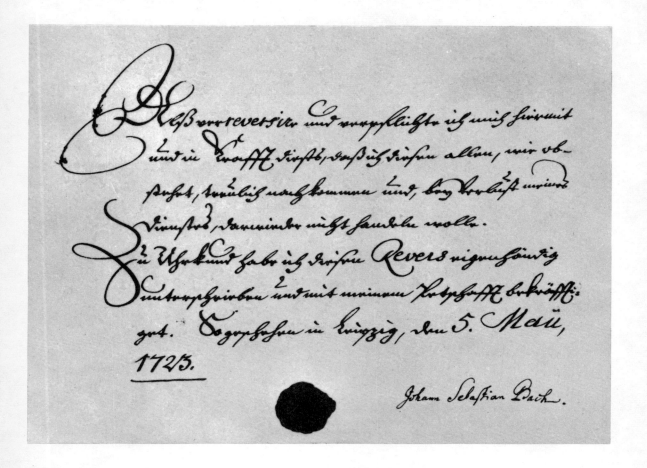

'his composition was much praised by those who like this kind of music'.

Meanwhile, Bach had gone back to Köthen. The decision for which he was waiting had really been made when it became clear that Graupner was definitely not coming, and the council's attitude towards Bach became more friendly on receipt of favourable reports about the *Hofkapellmeister* in Köthen. In the decisive council meeting of April 22 it was stated that 'one could even forget Telemann's behaviour if Bach was elected'.

Bach is elected   The council, having learnt by bitter experience, asked Bach to sign a document on April 19, in which he had to declare his readiness to do his duty according to the rules if he was elected. He also had to produce his certificate of

Last page of the contract
of May 5, 1723 and
Bach's signature

Superintendent
Salomon Deyling,
the composer's superior
at the Thomaskirche

dismissal signed by the Prince of Köthen. On May 5 he was officially informed
of his nomination, and the final contract was presented to him in the council
chambers for signature. His duties were laid down with a petty precision in
fourteen points, and thus the seed was sown for later quarrels. On May 13 he
called on the superintendent, Salomon Deyling, who examined his religious
beliefs, and made him sign a declaration of adherence to the Lutheran faith.

Bach then hurried back to his family, and the move to Leipzig took place on
May 22. The whole town showed an interest in this event and one North German newspaper described it in great detail: 'Last Saturday at noon, four carts
laden with goods and chattels belonging to the former *Kapellmeister* to the

On the list of teachers at St Thomas's the name of Johann Kuhnau, Cantor, is deleted and Johann Sebastian Bach is substituted in the margin

Evidence of Bach's first appearance in Leipzig: the receipt for his fee for testing an organ in December 1717

The Thomaskirche seen from the north

court of Köthen arrived in Leipzig where he had been nominated as Cantor of St Thomas's. At two in the afternoon he and his family arrived in two coaches and moved into their newly decorated lodgings in the school building'.

The Bach family then comprised his wife and four children, aged eight, nine, twelve and fourteen. The goods and chattels consisted of the usual household furniture plus several keyboard and other instruments.

On May 31 followed the inaugural ceremony with the customary speeches and anthems, putting an end to six unsettled months. From now on Bach was to play an important part in the cultural life of Leipzig. A golden age of music had begun within the walls of this university town, but the councillors, only too happy to have solved their problems somehow, must have been quite unaware of this development.

At this time, Leipzig had about 30,000 inhabitants. Bach knew the town from previous visits: he had come, for instance, in December 1717 to test the organ in the University church built by the Leipzig master Johann Scheibe. Bach's expert and detailed testimonial, including a plea for the underpaid organ-builder, must have attracted no less attention than his virtuosity when he played the organ during the service of dedication. He must have been pleased with this instrument since he liked to play on it even in later years. On this particular occasion Bach was presumably the guest of Kuhnau, his predecessor. The two men had met the year before while testing an organ at Halle, and Kuhnau may have recommended Bach as an expert to the Leipzig authorities.

The city had at that time many attractions for the summer holiday-makers. The neighbouring countryside and the well cared-for parks and pleasure gardens beside the river Pleisse constituted idyllic surroundings. The massive tower

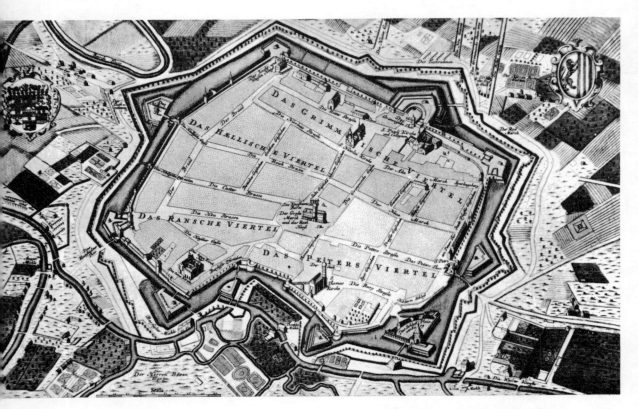

Town plan of Leipzig in 1723.

(Opposite) St Thomas's church and school in 1723

1. Die St. Thomas Kirche, 2. Die Thomas Schule.
3. Der Steinerne Waßer=Kasten.

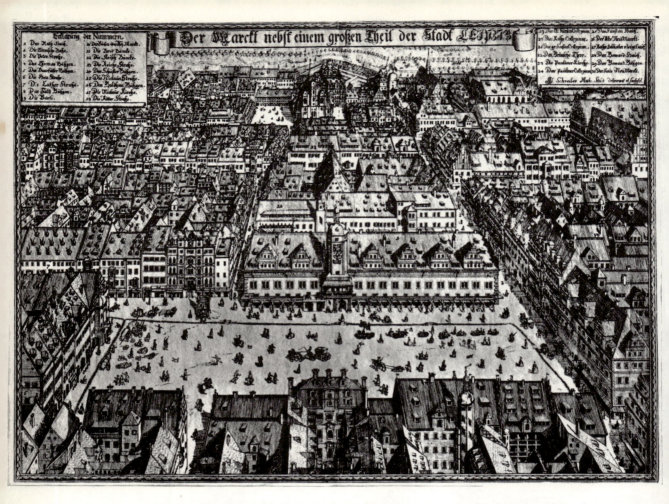

The market-place of Leipzig in the early 18th century. In the foreground on the right: the Thomasgasse

of the Pleissenburg rose above the city walls; these enclosed streets properly paved and illuminated during the night, magnificent private dwellings, coffee houses, inns, and the recently opened municipal libraries, the majestic town hall and numerous city churches. Scholars and learned men of distinction came from far and wide to the old-established University, and the famous book trade contributed much to the cultural life of the city.

One of Leipzig's most important features was its international commerce. While the fair was in progress, the respectable town was transformed into a show-ground, with a number of exotic side-shows popular also with members

The 'Thomaspförtchen', or little St Thomas gate, with church and school in the 18th century

of the royal court. Many connections were established between nations on these occasions, and this in turn had a beneficial effect on the city's commerce, as well as on its cultural activities.

Bach came to this lively town, nicknamed 'Athens on the Pleisse', with mixed feelings. He regarded the step from director of court music to civic cantor as a social come-down; on the other hand he was proud to play so important a part in one of the foremost centres of German cultural life. Besides, his decision to apply for this post had also been influenced by the thought that in Leipzig he could give his growing sons the education which he had been denied. As soon

St Thomas's School and the Thomaspförtchen towards the end of the 19th century. In the foreground, the monument to Bach presented by Mendelssohn. The old school building in which the composer lived was demolished in 1902. One of the windows on the first floor belonged to the composer's study

The plaque commemorating the demolished school building, and the composer; it did not endure, but was soon melted down

An dieser Stelle stand bis zum Jahre 1902 die alte Thomasschule In ihr wohnte und wirkte Meister Joh. Seb. Bach 1723-1750 Zum 185 Todestag am 28 Feuer 1935

as he had established himself, he had Friedemann, who was then only thirteen years old, put down for the University.

The School of St Thomas was situated near the western wall of the town, not far from the Pleissenburg. The way to the square, formerly the cemetery of St Thomas, led through the Thomaspförtchen (little St Thomas gate). This area, St Thomas's School with a fine fountain in the middle, was to be Bach's home ground for twenty-seven years. The northern and western sides of the square were bounded by the church and the school. The space in the southern wing of the sixteenth-century school building had become quite inadequate, for it contained, apart from the classrooms, dormitories and general rooms of the scholars, the living quarters of the rector or headmaster, and those of the cantor, which were divided between the ground floor and the next two storeys. *St Thomas's school*

From the *Componirstube*, the study on the first floor, there was a magnificent view of the surrounding gardens, fields and meadows. When the school was enlarged during the years 1731–32, and inaugurated on June 5, with Bach's cantata *Froher Tag, verlangte Stunden*, his home remained on the whole unaltered, and the town council was ill-advised to have this historic building demolished in 1902.

In the atmosphere of aristocratic ease at the court of Köthen, Bach could make music when and as he liked; here in Leipzig he had to adhere strictly to his duties within the highly organized life of church and school. A considerable readjustment in the composer's way of life was therefore inevitable, nor was

The Nicolaikirche in which Bach performed his first cantata as cantor

Signature to a testimonial
given by Bach in 1727

Bach divided his choristers into four groups

Bach's opinion of some of his choirboys (The last sentence is quoted in the text)

there any time for musing. Eight days after his arrival, on the first Sunday after Trinity, he directed his first cantata *Die Elenden sollen essen* in the Nicolaikirche, the city's principal church. This great and solemn cantata, to be performed in two parts, before and after the sermon, made a profound impression on the citizens of Leipzig. All the four voices were given recitatives and arias with varying instrumental accompaniment, the same melody was treated chorally as well as instrumentally and the opening movement consisted of a pensive choral prelude folowed by a lively choral fugue — it was indeed a masterly composition.

During the previous week Bach had auditioned and reorganized his choir of fifty-five boys. Only by the exercise of strict order and discipline was it possible to perform all the duties, and for a long time the choristers had been over-burdened with work, which included regular cantata and motet performances in the four main churches, weddings, funerals, New Year services and travelling. A list in Bach's own hand shows that for the four simultaneous Sunday services there were at best twelve boys available, three for each part, and as to

Auf Hochedl. und Hochweisen Hochlöbl. Raths Verordnung
hat dero Stadt Pfeiffer bißheriger Geselle,
Carl Friedrich Pfaffe in Gegenwart derer andern
Stadt Musicorum seine verlangte Probe abgeleget,
da sich denn befunden, daß er auf jedem Instru-
mente so von denen Stadtpfeiffern pfleget gebrau-
chet zu werden, als Violine, Hautbois, Flute Travers,
Trompette, Waldhorn und übrigen Baß Instrumenten,
schön Beyfall allers anhörenden gantz wohl hat
hören laßen, und der gesuchten Adjunctur gantz
geschickt befunden worden. Leipzig. d. 24. July.
1745.
Joh: Sebast: Bach.

Interior of the Thomaskirche (before the renovation in 1885)

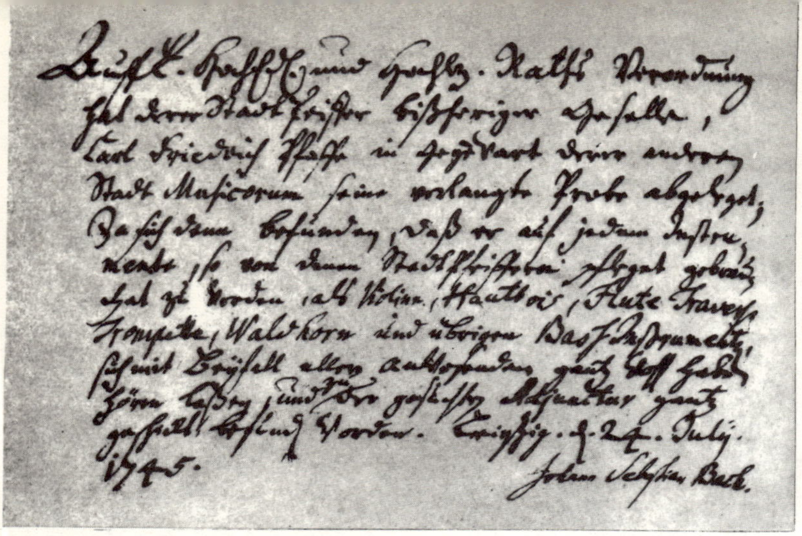

Testimonial (quoted in the text) certifying a journeyman town piper's proficiency on half a dozen instruments

their capability he wrote: 'In these three churches, namely St Thomas, St Nicolai and the Neukirche, all choristers must be musical. The rest, who do not understand music and can barely sing a chorale, go to the Peterskirche.' But even in the churches to which the 'musical' boys were allocated, the conditions were by no means always ideal. Bach had divided the choir into groups of singers: 'Seventeen good ones, twenty not yet ready and seventeen incapable', although for this inaugural cantata Bach must have had twelve highly gifted choristers because the vocal parts are full of difficulties. Apart from the choral movements sung by all the boys, there were solo parts for the leaders of each group of three, called the 'concertists'. Only for the soprano or contralto parts in a few solo cantatas or in the big choral works, Bach might have made use of

Daß Vorzeiger dieses H. Johann Christoph Altnickol
seit Michaelis ao. 1745. dem Choro Musico unausge-
setzt assistiret, indem er bald als Violiste, bald als
Violoncelliste, meistens aber als Vocal-Bassiste sich
exhibiret, und also dem Mangel derer auf der Tho-
mas-Schule sich befindenden Baß-Stimmen (weilen
sie wegen allzu frühzeitigen Abzugs nicht können zur
Reiffe kommen) ersetzet; Wird hiermit eigenhändig
bezeuget. Leipzig. d. 25. Maji. 1747.
Joh: Sebast: Bach.

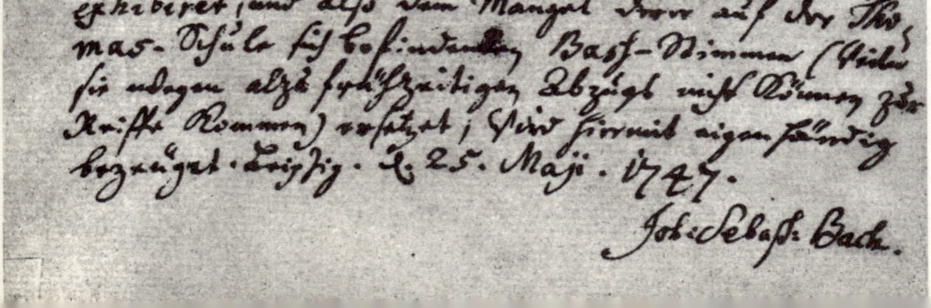

Testimonial for the student Altnikol, Bach's future son-in-law, who was of assistance to him in the choir and orchestra

Bach's virtuoso trumpeter Gottfried Reiche,
member of the Leipzig 'municipal orchestra'.
The composer wrote many trumpet parts for him

students able to sing with a falsetto voice, producing a sound not unlike that of
a counter-tenor.

The 'municipal orchestra' was not big enough for the accompaniment of cantatas, for which at least twelve players were needed. Only four town pipers, *Bach's orchestra*
three violinists and one apprentice were available, but Bach could count on these *in Leipzig*
musicians who were always ready to help even if their actual performance was
not always on the highest level. Their life was full of hardship and they were
forever looking for casual work to supplement their meagre income. 'Some of
them were often so harassed by worries about their daily bread that their
musicianship necessarily suffered.' In one way, however, they were more useful
than orchestral musicians of to-day: they were able to play several instruments.
Bach certified on July 24, 1745 that one town piper 'was proficient on all the
usual instruments, namely the violin, the oboe, the transverse flute, the trumpet,
the horn and the rest of the bass instruments'.

Fortunately there were some outstanding musicians among these players.
The greatest of them was the trumpeter Gottfried Reiche, and his portrait is
one of the most beautiful pictures of a musician in the eighteenth century. His
extraordinary virtuosity is illustrated not only by the difficult fanfare which he
is shown here holding in his hand, but above all by the numerous brilliant
trumpet passages evidently specially written for him by Bach. The trumpeters

Flute part of an aria from a cantata

of modern times, having lost the art of 'clarino playing', find these parts very difficult. Some students or advanced pupils were no doubt used to augmenting the little orchestra, otherwise Bach would never have written so elaborate a score for his first cantata. Only a few rehearsals were available to prepare this motley ensemble for the new cantata style which was henceforth to be that of the Thomaskirche.

To follow this first work, Bach wrote the very similar cantata *Die Himmel erzählen die Ehre Gottes* for the second Sunday after Trinity. Eventually there was a cantata for every Sunday, except during Lent and Advent, and week after week for years on end the routine work of composing, writing out parts, rehearsing and performing remained the same. Only occasionally did Bach make use of earlier compositions in their original form or in new arrangements.

Sometimes there were solo cantatas accompanied by only a few instruments; at other times the choir had the most important part, but almost every cantata finished with a simple chorale, in which Bach used the four voices so expressively that the term 'Bach chorale' has gained general currency.

At that time Bach also worked the more elaborate choral modes into his cantatas. We must surely regard as his supreme achievement the composition of countless choral cantatas by means of freely paraphrasing the middle verses of hymns and adapting them to recitative and aria form. The beginning and the end were treated as two choral movements, the first taking a highly developed form, the last being a simple chorale. In this way a new, unified composition was achieved, combining the spirit of the old choral partita with modern ideas.

Bach's music cabinet contained great stacks of cantata scores and parts, all very tidy and carefully classified. In the end there were five complete annual cycles in systematic order, and though only three-fifths of the music is pre-

Final words of a great number of compositions: 'Fine. Soli Deo Gloria'.

When the rector of St Thomas's, J. H. Ernesti, died in 1729, Bach wrote for him the funeral motet *Der Geist hilft unsrer Schwachheit auf*

served to-day, this substantial portion is enough to give us a good idea of Bach's productivity during his first few years at Leipzig, particularly if one remembers that he wrote numerous other vocal compositions — above all, the motets — during that same period.

After only a few weeks in Leipzig, Bach was commissioned to write a funeral motet for five voices for 'the Postmaster's widow Mrs Keess', a lady hardly known to him. If the occasion is of little consequence, the work itself, entitled *Jesu meine Freude*, is one of the most famous choral compositions of all time. Similar in character is the funeral motet in eight parts *Fürchte Dich nicht*, written in 1726, and the motet of 1729 for double choir composed in honour of the rector of St Thomas's, Johann Heinrich Ernesti, called *Der Geist hilft unsrer Schwachheit auf*. To this creative phase belongs also the motet *Singet dem Herrn*, whose exultant strains were to affect so deeply not only Mozart but generations of Bach enthusiasts. To-day these compositions are not regarded any more as purely a *capella* works, but even judging from performances with instrumental accompaniment, the ability of Bach's choir is evident. On these occasions he had the whole choir at his disposal.

Apart from his duties as cantor at St Thomas's, Bach took a lively interest in the music for the divine service at the Paulinerkirche. It took eleven performances directed by him before Christmas 1725, for him to realize that he was trespassing on the grounds of the University authorities. He had honestly believed that the traditional rule, making the cantor of St Thomas's automatically director of music at the University, was still in force, but during the interim period after Kuhnau's death the academic authorities had appointed Görner, the but moderately talented organist at the Nicolaikirche, to this post. A temporary solution was found: Bach was to retain the so-called 'old Divine Service' (performed during the three major church festivals, also on Reformation day and during the academic quarter day celebrations), while Görner was given the 'new Divine Service' (on ordinary Sundays). This arrangement did not suit Bach at all, and one of the reasons why he opposed it was the loss of income it entailed. He therefore continued to fight for his rights and even appealed to the King. Eventually a compromise was reached, but the disappointed Bach gradually withdrew from the musical activities of the University, a development for which the authorities themselves were to blame. They had decided to rely upon a mediocre musician whose works are to-day forgotten, and so they missed the chance of fostering a great development in academic music.

From then on, Bach gave his services to the University only on certain special occasions. One such was the academic funeral service on October 17, 1727 for the deceased Christiane Eberhardine, wife of the Elector. In this particular case the private sponsor was an aristocrat student who had specified Gottsched as poet and Bach as composer. Significantly, the University and also the 'aca-

demic director of music' Görner, protested strongly, and only shortage of time prevented the arrangements from being cancelled. Bach's magnificent and moving setting for the funeral ode, *Lass, Fürstin, lass noch einen Strahl* betrays nothing of the unpleasant circumstances under which this composition was written.

It was not until he was asked to become the permanent director of the '*collegium musicum*', founded in 1729 by Telemann, that Bach received official recognition of the high regard in which he was held. He had previously helped this students' ensemble on several occasions; for the next ten years he was to compose a great number of occasional works specifically for this group. Sometimes the private performances by these students were given in honour of a famous university professor, when they included a specially commissioned composition. For example, in 1725 Bach wrote for the saint's day of August

Friedrich Müller, Professor of Philosophy, the humorous *Äoluskantate*, and in the following year the cantata *Vereinigte Zwietracht der wechselnden Saiten* to celebrate the nomination of Dr Gottlieb Korte as Professor of Jurisprudence. Finally, in 1735 a member of the scholarly Rivinus family from Leipzig was honoured by the cantata *Die Freude reget sich*.

Bach also provided music for commemorative occasions at the court. Performances of this kind were usually sponsored by well-to-do students from the nobility, or the middle classes, and contributions were collected by means of a subscription list put up on the notice board. In this way the quite considerable costs of such an undertaking — torchlight illumination, printing, etc. — were covered. These serenades provided a substantial income for the composer, as the receipts in the University archives show. On May 5, 1738 Bach wrote such a receipt for fifty-eight thalers: fifty for himself and eight for the town pipers who had augmented the orchestra. This sum represented the fee for the cantata *Willkommen, ihr herrschenden Götter der Erden*. Unfortunately nothing more than the text has been preserved.

The royal birthdays and saints' days were celebrated with such performances. There were two birthday cantatas in 1733: one, *Hercules auf dem Scheidewege*, for the Prince Elector, and *Tönet, ihr Pauken, erschallet, Trompeten* for the Queen. Bach took the ten best movements from these cantatas and incorporated them in the Christmas Oratorio.

The anniversary of the King's election on October 5, 1734 was celebrated with pomp and circumstance in true Baroque style. At that time the royal court was at Leipzig for the Michaelmas Fair:

'In the evening at seven a cannon was fired and the whole town illuminated . . . At about nine in the evening the resident students humbly presented a serenade with trumpets and drums to His Majesty, composed by Mr Joh. Bach, Capellmeister and Cantor at St Thomas's. Six hundred students carried wax torches, and four counts acted as marshals, leading the music . . . When the composition was presented the four counts were graciously permitted to kiss His Majesty's hand. The King, the Queen, and the Princes did not leave the window but listened to the music with great pleasure as long as it lasted.'

But the festivities finished on a sad note: Bach lost his trumpeter Gottfried Reiche, who died of a sudden stroke 'because he had strained himself on the previous day playing for the royal celebrations, and the smoke of the torches had given him trouble'.

During 1733 and 1734 Bach wrote a remarkably quick succession of compositions in honour of the court at Dresden, hoping that this would encourage the

In memory of the Elector's
wife Christiane Eberhardine
(right), who died in 1727,
Bach composed the music, and
Gottsched (below) wrote the
words for a funeral ode

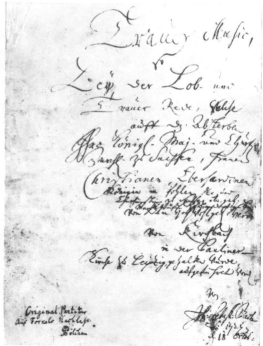

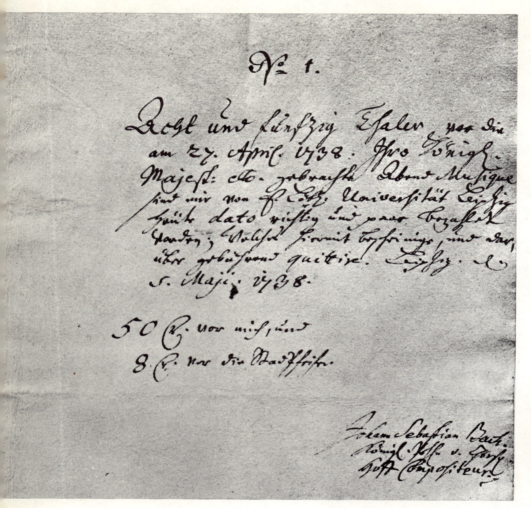

Receipt for a fee in Bach's handwriting: '50 thalers for me and 8 thalers for the town pipers'

Elector to give him a court appointment. This, he thought, would improve his professional standing in Leipzig. The new Elector had only been in office for a few months when Bach, on July 27, 1733, sent the parts for a Kyrie and a Gloria — both new compositions later to be incorporated in the *B minor Mass* — together with a letter asking the Prince to grant him his patronage. Bach's problems were quite clear — the professional unpleasantness which had led to

In the autumn of 1734 Bach composed
music for the anniversary of Frederick
Augustus II's election to the throne of Poland
(as Augustus III)

a diminution of his fees. The Dresden honour would strengthen his hand in his
struggles with the Leipzig authorities. Although the issue of such a decree was
delayed until November 19, 1736 because of involvement in hostilities and
political troubles of various kinds, it still arrived in time to offer Bach protection
against those who sought to slight him. After the trouble with the University
there followed quarrels with the church council over the choice of anthems;

Bass part of the Gloria of the *B minor Mass* in Bach's handwriting

later, endless battles had to be fought with the civic authorities and the school board. Bach had to battle continuously for his rights. His artistic freedom, above all, was constantly imperilled by attacks from the various councils with their pedantic regulations.

Music in school and church had suffered through the introduction of unreasonable measures by the authorities, and this only helped to increase the tension. Unmusical boys were accepted as pupils in the school, with the result that the choir deteriorated. The usual subsidies for students assisting in the performances were cut, and the seven town pipers, whose situation was desperate, received no official assistance.

On August 23, 1730 Bach severely took the town council of Leipzig to task. This 'short but most necessary plan for the establishment of a proper church music' is in the nature of an indictment, in which he ruthlessly pointed out how inefficient was the management of the municipal music, while stressing the shortage of singers as well as the poor quality of the available musicians.

The council in turn blamed Bach for this state of affairs, and their reproach was not unreasonable where his duties at the school were concerned. Bach was no ideal schoolmaster. By contract he was supposed to teach Latin, but he managed very quickly to pass this duty on to a junior colleague. His singing lessons must have been given in a rather haphazard way since, when he needed

In a letter accompanying the parts of the *Kyrie and Gloria in B minor* which he sent to the court in Dresden, Bach asked to be given a court appointment

lich nachbleiben möchte, dahero Ew. Königl.
Hoheit mir die Gnade erweisen und ein Praedicat
von Dero Hoff-Capelle conferiren, und deswegen
zu Ertheilung eines Decrets, gehörigen Orths Hohen
Befehl ergehen laßen würden; Solche gnädigste Ge-
wehrung meiner unterthänigsten Bitte wird mich zu
unendlicher Verehrung verbinden und ich offerire
mich in schuldigsten Gehorsam, iedesmahl auch
Ew. Königl. Hoheit gnädigstem Verlangen, in Com-
ponirung der Kirchen Musique, sowohl als zum
Orchestre meinen unermüdeten Fleiß zu erweisen
und meine gantze Kräffte zu Dero Dienste
zuzuwenden, in unaußhörlicher Treue verharrend

Ew. Königl. Hoheit

Dreßden
den 27. Julij
1733.

unterthänigst-gehor-
samster Knecht

Johann Sebastian Bach.

Bach's friend Gesner was rector at St Thomas's School from 1730 to 1734

a continuous period of work for a major composition, he sometimes did not appear. Besides, the behaviour of schoolchildren in Bach's time was shockingly bad, and teaching them must have given him little pleasure.

The city council was, of course, unable to understand problems of this kind and Bach was told in no uncertain terms that 'not only did the cantor fail to do his duty, but he would not even try to justify himself; nor did he teach singing properly. Other complaints had been made besides. There would have to be an improvement since to continue in this way was impossible.' They also decided 'to reduce the Cantor's salary . . . because he was incorrigible'.

Bach might have reconciled himself to the inability of the council to understand artistic matters, but the attempt to reduce his income made him really furious, and he began to look for another appointment. On October 28, 1730 he wrote a letter to his friend Erdmann in Danzig, asking him to find him a 'convenient post', so that he might escape from the 'trouble, envy and persecution' he had perpetually to face in Leipzig. The city would have lost Bach if a great friend and admirer had not just then come to his aid. Johann Matthias Gesner, who had known the composer since his Weimar days, had become headmaster of St Thomas's School. He used his influence to improve the situation generally, and to secure better working conditions for Bach. However, when Gesner accepted a nomination of the University of Göttingen only four years later, Bach's opponents renewed their campaign.

The summer of 1736 saw the beginning of a quarrel to which a big bundle of documents bear witness. For two years both sides fought bitterly for the right to appoint a prefect to a vacant position. The music at St Thomas's suffered severely as a result, and the new rector Johann August Ernesti made matters worse by inciting the scholars against the cantor, who had no alternative but to appeal to the throne. He asked the Prince to issue an order to the church council demanding an apology from Ernesti, and to request Superintendent

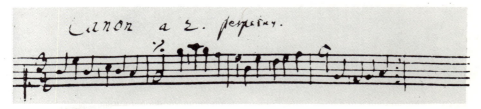

In 1734 Bach dedicated a canon to Gesner

Bach fought tenaciously for his rights in repeated petitions to the authorities

The rector of St Thomas's,
J. A. Ernesti, opposed Bach in his
musical work at school

Deyling to admonish the school so that the cantor would be respected and obeyed. In the meantime Bach had been nominated 'composer to the court', and as a result of this support given by the sovereign his authority was restored; all the same, this disturbing sequence of events must have taken all the pleasure out of his work.

Nevertheless, the number of scores in Bach's music cabinet grew even in these critical years. If the council had pointed out that he showed little inclination to work, work he did in his own way; numerous compositions date from this time. During the first six years in Leipzig he had composed a vast amount of church music, but after 1729 he concentrated on instrumental works and homage cantatas written mostly for the *collegium musicum;* the output of new church-cantatas was very small.

At the beginning and the end of his first creative period Bach composed his two major works of Protestant choral music: The *Passions according to St John* and *St Matthew*. Both were revised several times on later occasions.

One of the greatest choral works of his second period was the *Christmas Oratorio*, whose six component cantatas were performed on the six Sundays of

ORATORIUM,
Welches
Die heilige Weyhnacht
über
In beyden
Haupt-Kirchen
zu Leipzig
musiciret wurde.
ANNO 1734.

Title page of the *Christmas Oratorio*
printed in 1734

the Christmas cycle in 1734–35. It is significant that the arias and choral movements of this work were almost without exception taken from secular compositions after the text had been changed.

Any account of Bach's musical life would be incomplete without a reference to the surroundings which probably quickened his creative genius more than any other place: his own home in the St Thomas's school building. The big room on the first floor was presumably the music room, as it contained the instruments listed among his belongings after his death. There were no less than six keyboard instruments: the possibilities for chamber music were thus inexhaustible. This music-making at home must have been at its best from 1730 onwards. The two eldest sons, taught by their father, had become good musi-

First text page
of the *Christmas Oratorio* (1734)

cians in their own right. Bach said in a letter of that time: 'They are really born musicians, and I can safely say that a good vocal and instrumental concert can be performed by my family, as my present wife has a very fine soprano voice and my daughter's progress is gratifying.'

After his wife Anna Magdalena and their eldest daughter Catharina Dorothea, Bach preferred his sons Wilhelm Friedemann and Carl Philipp Emanuel as musical partners. Together with them he played the *Concerti for several Cembali* which were transcribed from other instrumental concertos during this period. They are the forerunners of the concerto for pianoforte. Advanced students or pupils gladly played the orchestral parts on these occasions, and there was always an open house for travelling musicians and virtuosi, who did not want to miss the chance, so Philipp Emanuel reported later, to make the acquaintance of the famous court composer and to be inspired by his performance, or to play to him. Thus Bach's home must have been one of the most important centres of the musical world.

Another musical centre was Zimmermann's coffee house in the Katharinen-strasse. Every week the *collegium musicum* met there to play under Bach's direction, in the presence of an interested public. In the summer the meetings took place during the afternoon in the garden, and in the winter evenings they were held in the coffee rooms. At the time of the trade fair in particular many music-lovers and amateurs came to listen, and the owner of the coffee house, with an eye to business, acted as concert agent who provided the instruments and paid the fees to the performers. Many of Bach's orchestral and chamber

Bach's son Philipp Emanuel
(1714–1788)

music compositions presumably had their first performance there, but works by other composers, particularly the music from fashionable operas, must have been performed as well, whilst guest artists, on their way through Leipzig, would have provided a welcome change. These concerts were one of the many contributory sources of his income. Compositions to celebrate a special occasion were very well paid. Perhaps that delightful satire on the current vogue of coffee drinking among the ladies of Leipzig, *The Coffee Cantata*, was inspired by these surroundings. Even in later years Bach used every opportunity to write such occasional compositions. During August 1742 he went with a small group of musicians to Kleinzschocher to pay homage to the new lord of the manor, the district councillor and chamberlain Carl Heinrich von Dieskau. The resulting libretto was provided by the resident poet Picander, and apart from a good

Bach's son Wilhelm Friedemann
(1710–1784)

Dresden in the
18th century

deal of bucolic humour and frivolity, it contained some daring words of criticism. The orchestration is that of a genuine village band at a country fair, and the mixture of arias, dances and folksongs followed the age-old tradition of travelling musicians.

The scope for occasional compositions was confined to Leipzig and the surrounding districts, but Bach gladly accepted any commission to test or dedicate a new organ as far afield as Saxony or even Thuringia. He liked to spend some time in Dresden, where the splendid buildings of Daniel Pöppelmann and Georg Bähr, built during the earlier part of the century, determined the character of the city. The Zwinger, the Augustus Bridge and the Frauenkirche must

have impressed him as much as the court orchestra which included a number of famous musicians. As early as 1730 Bach wrote a memorandum comparing the achievements of this group to the pitiful conditions in Leipzig.

The conductor of the Dresden Opera, Johann Adolf Hasse, and his wife were great friends of Bach's, and they visited one another on several occasions. In 1731 Bach went to Dresden to hear Hasse's opera *Cleofide*, and after the performance he gave a very successful recital of organ music in the Sophien-kirche. A Dresden newspaper wrote the following poem in his honour:

> Although a brook is pleasant to the ear,
> The while it spills through field and rocky cleft,

Bach played on these famous Silbermann organs in Dresden:
the organ of the Sophienkirche (above), and that of the Frauenkirche (right)

Square in front of the Frauenkirche in Dresden in the 18th century
Title page of the *Clavir-Übung I*, published by the composer in 1731

Far nobler is the Brook* whom you can hear
Address the keys with fingers wondrous deft.
'Tis said, When Orpheus used to pluck the strings
The forest creatures meekly to him came,
But when our own Bach's music richly rings,
He puts great Orpheus himself to shame.

Bach's success must have had some bearing on Wilhelm Friedemann's appointment in 1733 to the post of organist in the Sophienkirche. Three years later Johann Sebastian received a similar ovation when, having been appointed composer to the court of Saxony, he gave a concert lasting two hours to celebrate the occasion on the Silbermann organ in the Frauenkirche. The enlightened society of Dresden must have made him feel at home whenever he came to the city.

The last period of Bach's life, starting about 1736, was dedicated to the task of perfecting, assembling and collating his works. *The Passions According to St John* and *St Matthew* were moulded into their final shape and so were several cantatas. The Kyrie and Gloria became the principal movements of the gigantic *B minor Mass*. A second part was added to the *Wohltemperierte Klavier*, six cantata movements were arranged as chorales for organ, and seventeen other compositions of the same kind were collected in one volume.

At the same time Bach was working on the systematic publication of instructive keyboard compositions, and eventually he published four parts of the *Clavir-Übung*. Six partitas appeared in 1731, *The Italian Concerto* and the great *B minor Overture* in 1735, and in 1739, as the third part, the volume of collected choral preludes sometimes called the 'Organ Mass'. Finally, in 1742 the fourth part was published containing the great cycle of the *Goldberg Variations*, the touchstone of all his keyboard works. The theme of these variations was taken from a saraband in Anna Magdalena's music book, and the work was commissioned by a patron, the Count von Keyserlingk, Russian ambassador to the court of Saxony, who employed the Bach pupil and cembalo player Goldberg. Forkel reported as follows on the curious origin of this occasional composition:

'The Count once said that he would like Bach to write a few gentle and happy pieces which his cembalo player Goldberg could play to cheer him up during his sleepless nights. The composer thought that a set of variations was best suited for this purpose, although he had never written variations before,

*The German for 'brook' is Bach (Transl.)

and had always considered this kind of composition a thankless task because
the basic harmony never changed . . . this is the only example of this kind of
music he ever wrote. Hereafter the count always called it his own, and for a
long time to come he said when he could not sleep at night: 'Dear Goldberg,
please play one of my variations to me." Bach has perhaps never received so
generous a reward for any other work.'

Bach wrote a second cycle of variations on the Christmas Chorale *Vom
Himmel hoch, da komm ich her* when he joined the 'Society of Musical Studies'
in Leipzig, whose aim was to explore the rational basis of music. The founder
and director, Lorenz Mizler, one of Bach's pupils, had been trying for a long
time to interest his teacher in this society which counted Handel and Telemann
among its members.

When Bach at last accepted the nomination in 1747 he was obliged to have
his portrait painted and to present it to the library. This picture was executed
by the official painter to the court and council, Elias Gottlieb Hausmann. It
shows the cantor of St Thomas's holding a sheet of music with a triple canon
in six parts, thus demonstrating his importance as a composer.

A significant event during the last years of Bach's life was his visit in May
1747 to Frederick II, King of Prussia. Music was the King's favourite pastime:
he was an enthusiastic flute-player and even a modest composer, but only
music written in the fashionable Italian style was of real interest to him, and
the excellent musicians of his chamber ensemble were not always happy in the
service of their selfish and dictatorial royal master.

Bach's son Carl Philipp Emanuel was employed in this ensemble as cembalo
player. When he had finished studying law in Leipzig and Frankfurt he moved
to Berlin, but he could not have felt at ease for long in this narrow-minded
atmosphere, particularly since his honest character often prompted him to speak
his mind, and for this reason he could hardly have been a favourite of the
King. Nevertheless he must have arranged the meeting between Frederick and
his father, but it is likely that Bach's patron, the Count von Keyserlingk, who
had meanwhile become ambassador to the court of Prussia, used his influence
on behalf of the composer.

But it never amounted to a formal invitation. The reason for Bach's journey,
delayed by the war between Prussia and Saxony, was purely a family visit: he
wanted to see his daughter-in-law and his first grandchild. He was joined in

Frederick II (the Great), King of
Prussia, was visited by Bach
in May 1747. He gave the composer
a theme to improvise upon,
which later became the theme
for the *Musical Offering*

Halle by Wilhelm Friedemann, who had gone there from Dresden when he was
appointed organist at the Marienkirche. It is not known how the visit to the
King in Potsdam came about.

At all events, on the evening of May 7 the two great men met. The King
interrupted his flute-playing to welcome the 'old Bach' affably. Then he invited
him to try his new keyboard instrument by Silbermann, giving him a theme
to improvise upon. Both sons have given accounts of this episode, though
later these were distorted and dramatized. The King was presumably incapable
of understanding Bach's genius because of the great difference in the musical
tastes of the two men.

However, Bach was confident that the King was favourably disposed towards him, for, when he returned home, he resolved to make use of the improvisation for a more permanent composition. With extraordinary rapidity he developed a ricercare in three parts, a canonic fugue and several canons from the theme, and sent the engraved music as a *Musical Offering*, together with a humble dedication, to the King. He later added some more canons, the famous ricercare in six parts and, as a further compliment to the King, a Trio Sonata including a flute part. The structural form of this rich and mysterious polyphonic work was not properly understood until recent times.

The *Musical Offering* was, so to speak, the overture to a still greater miracle of polyphony, *The Art of Fugue*, and this composition occupied the last months of his life. It was his intention to discover every possible mutation of which a musical theme was capable, and so create a concentrated work of instruction on the fugue, the musical form so characteristic of his art. *The Art of Fugue* is by no means a work of academic rules but a living composition in which the artistry of the thematic integration is beyond belief. In the final quadruple fugue, at the point where the theme B A C H is introduced, and the parts are dissolved in a surprising way leaving one voice which seems to toss a question into the void, Carl Philipp Emanuel has written: 'While engaged on this

One of the keyboard instruments made by Silbermann belonging to
Frederick the Great

A page from the score in the first printed edition of the *Musical Offering* (1747)

fugue, in which the name B A C H is used as a counter-subject, the composer died.' (See footnote on page 34.)

It took people a long time to realize that with this composition Bach had created one of the greatest works in the history of Western music, and to rate it at its true value. It has since become an indispensable part of every serious musician's education.

The last year of Bach's life was overshadowed by many worries, but no doubt his daughter Elisabeth's wedding to the Naumburg organist and Bach pupil Altnikol, and the brilliant development of his talented youngest son Johann Christian provided some consolation. His eyes were seriously affected by a malady caused through overworking in a poor light, and this in turn began to undermine his general health. As early as May 1749 his illness must have reached rather an advanced stage, and the powerful minister Brühl in Dresden must have been aware of this, because he sent a message to the Leipzig council sug-

The page of *The Art of Fugue* on which Carl Philipp Emanuel's annotation appears

gesting one of his protégés, the orchestral director Johann Gottlieb Harrer, as cantor in the event of Bach's death. The council arranged an audition as early as June 8, and the city records say that he was enthusiastically nominated 'future cantor of St Thomas's, if the present cantor and Capellmeister Mr Sebastian Bach should die.'

Bach on his sickbed must have heard some news about Harrer. Fury and defiance gave him new strength, and it was perhaps in such a state of mind that he made the desperate decision to put himself in the care of an English physician, who was on his way through Leipzig. Two operations were performed in March and April, and their weakening effect was so aggravated by harmful medicine that he became still more infirm. Despite the efforts of two very able doctors to save him, he died peacefully of a stroke followed by a severe fever on July 28, 1750 'in the evening, after a quarter to nine, in the sixty-sixth year of his life, yielding up his blessed soul to his saviour'.

He was buried in St John's cemetery outside the town in the early morning of July 31, and in the absence of any tombstone the position of his grave was soon forgotten.

Council and school were not really moved by the death of their cantor. The minutes of the council meeting on August 7 stated with insulting indifference: 'the cantor of the School of St Thomas, or rather the orchestral director Bach, has also died'. The malicious words of the mayor Dr Stieglitz, saying that the school was in need of a *Kapellmeister*, and not a cantor, betray his satisfaction in the belief that the musical affairs of the city could at last return to normal, now that this difficult man had disappeared from the scene.

There was, of course, great sadness in the family and among his friends. Georg Philipp Telemann became their spokesman when he composed a sonnet in honour of his deceased colleague:

> Lamented Bach! Your touch upon the organ's keys
> Long since has earned you company among the great,
> And what your quill upon the music-sheet has writ
> Has filled hearts with delight, though some did envy seize.
> Rest then! Your name is safe from time's extinguishing . . .

Anna Magdalena was worried about the future of her four young children. Although Bach's estate, as recorded in the Register, provided a moderate legacy, it had to be divided. One third went to the widow, and two thirds to the nine surviving children. The sum realized from the sale of effects was only sufficient to cover Anna's expenses for a few months. A petition to the council secured her the tenancy of Bach's home for another 'six months of grace', but at the end of this period she had to find accommodation with friends. Two years later she received from the city adminstration the sum of forty thalers; in return she handed some of her late husband's music to the council. She died on February 27, 1760 as 'almoner in the Haynstrasse'. Only the poorest of funeral services, the so-called 'quarter school' consisting of some bad chorale singing by three sopranos at her graveside, was vouchsafed this great artist and loyal helpmate of the cantor of St Thomas's, who also acted as his untiring copyist.

The greater part of Bach's innumerable manuscripts went to the two eldest sons, but they made little use of this material in the course of their career. Musical taste had undergone a considerable change. The sons themselves, searching for new modes of expression, necessarily had to break away from their father's tradition, but as musicians in their own right they carried the fame of their family name almost into the nineteenth century.

Several petitions show the courage of Anna Magdalena Bach in dealing with the difficulties arising from her husband's death. Her signature reads: 'Anna Magdalena Bach, widow'

Bach's youngest son Johann Christian died in 1782. He had spent the latter part of his life as music master to Queen Charlotte in London; his eldest brother Wilhelm Friedemann died two years later. He ended a distinguished though restless life as a poor man in Berlin. Carl Philipp Emanuel lived until 1788 in Hamburg, where he became director of church music, highly esteemed by everyone. Johann Christoph Friedrich finished his days as *Kapellmeister* to the court of Bückeburg in 1795.

Only the youngest child, the daughter Regina Susanna, lived to see the beginning of the great revival of her father's works in the next century. The music editor Rochlitz made a successful appeal in 1800 to the musicians of Germany for donations to support Bach's last surviving daughter who was living in poverty.

When she died in 1809, one book had already appeared which set in train the rediscovery of the composer's works: it was the Bach biography by the director of music at the University of Göttingen, Johann Nikolaus Forkel. This was the first occasion on which anyone had claimed for Bach that his works 'represented an invaluable national inheritance, such as no other nation could match'.

Bach's sarcophagus in the
vaults of the Johanniskirche
(until 1949)

Bach's last resting-place
in the Thomaskirche

Furthermore, he invited his readers to 'uphold the memory of this great man and to regard it as a national duty'.

By slow degrees musicologists, publishers and musicians of subsequent generations brought to light once more Bach's compositions, singly at first and later in the monumental edition of his collected works. By thus introducing these works to the public they paved the way for the Bach renaissance in the nineteenth century.

When the Johanniskirche was rebuilt in 1894 a few Leipzig scholars and Bach admirers succeeded in having what were believed to be the composer's bones exhumed. Partial identification was established by a series of anatomical and other tests. The bones were laid to rest once more in a stone coffin next to those of the poet Gellert, and many people went to pay homage at this tomb until the church was destroyed by bombs during the Second World War. Once more his remains were rescued and buried, this time in the chancel of the Thomaskirche. It is to be hoped that this will be their final resting-place.

The Thomaskirche is still the traditional centre for Bach's music, though meanwhile other places have also become important. Now musicologists have begun to piece together a new and authentic version of his life and works, and it is gratifying to note that most music-loving nations are taking part in this new effort.

For all of that, the greatness of his work will remain unfathomable. Perhaps only Beethoven's enthusiastic words do justice to his sublime stature and profundity: 'Not Brook but Ocean should be his name . . .'

Marble bust of Bach
by Carl Seffner

Seffner modelled Bach's
portrait bust on the
measurements of the skull

Living tradition: The spirit of the Cantor of St Thomas's lives on in the choir of St Thomas's

POSTSCRIPT

The purpose of this pictorial biography is to present Bach's life with the help of relevant pictures. Those who have accompanied me through its pages should, I suggest, add to this the experience of listening to the music itself — and then, perhaps, return to the book. It is particularly important to bear Bach's great music in mind when reading of his everyday life so hampered by provincial narrow-mindedness, since music cannot be properly described in words but must be heard.

The contents of this pictorial biography are based on the latest research; the pictures are mostly from my own collection to which have been added others kindly provided by various libraries, museums and archives, all acknowledged in the Notes on the pictures. I extend my sincere gratitude to them and to all who helped in the preparation of this book; above all may I thank my wife, to whom it is dedicated.

Werner Neumann

1685 March 21: Johann Sebastian Bach is born, youngest son of the court and town musician Johann Ambrosius Bach in Eisenach. Baptised on March 23 in the Georgenkirche.

1693–1695 Pupil of the Latin school in Eisenach.

1694 May 3: Funeral of his mother, Elisabeth (maiden name Lämmerhirt).

1695 February 24: Funeral of his father.

1695–1700 Bach is living with his eldest brother Johann Christoph in Ohrdruf and becomes a pupil of the Gymnasium there.

1700–1702 Choirboy of the Michaelis school in Lüneburg.

1703 March: Violinist in the chamber orchestra of Duke Johann Ernest of Sachsen-Weimar. August 9: Organist of the Neue Kirche in Arnstadt.

1704 Capriccio in B flat major for the departure of his brother Johann Jakob.

1705 Bach visits the great organist and composer, Dietrich Buxtehude, in Lübeck.

1706 February 21 and November 11: Inquiry of the Arnstadt church council.

1707 June 15: Organist at the Blasiuskirche in Mühlhausen. October 17: Marriage to his cousin Maria Barbara in the church at Dornheim.

1708 February 4: Performance of the cantata *Gott ist mein König* for the inauguration of the new council. June 25: Seeks acceptance of his resignation from the town council of Mühlhausen. July: Chamber musician and court organist to Wilhelm Ernst, Duke of Sachsen-Weimar.

1709 Reformation day: Bach in Mühlhausen (dedication of the organ).

1710 November 22: Birth of his son Wilhelm Friedemann.

1711 February 16: Bach's testimonial for the organ-builder, Heinrich Trebs.

1713 December 14: Offer of the post of organist at the Liebfrauenkirche in Halle.

1714 March 2: Nomination as leader of the court orchestra in Weimar. March 8: Birth of his son Carl Philipp Emanuel.

1715 May 11: Birth of his son Johann Gottfried Bernhard.

1716 February 23: Performance of the *Jagdkantate* in Weissenfels on the birthday of Duke Christian. April 28 to May 3: Organ-testing in the Liebfrauenkirche in Halle. July 31: Organ-testing in Erfurt.

1717 August 5: Kapellmeister and director of chamber music at the court of Prince Leopold of Anhalt-Köthen. September: Contest with Marchand in Dresden. November 6 to December 2: Placed under arrest by Duke Wilhelm Ernst. December 17: Tests and reports on the organ of the university church of St Pauli in Leipzig.

1718 May: Journey to Karlsbad with Prince Leopold.

1719 October: Vain attempt to meet Handel in Halle.

1720 January 22: Start of the *Clavir-Büchlein vor Wilhelm Friedemann Bach*. May to July: Journey to Karlsbad with Prince Leopold. July 7: Funeral of Maria Barbara. November: Journey to Hamburg and encounter with Jan Adams Reinken – now nearly a hundred – at the organ of the Katharinenkirche.

1721 March 24: Dedication of the six *Concerts avec plusieurs instruments* to the Margrave Christian Ludwig of Brandenburg. December 3: Second marriage, to Anna Magdalena Wilke.

1722 The first music book for Anna Magdalena Bach.

1723 February 7: Cantata audition for the post of Cantor of St Thomas's. April 13: Gracious dismissal from the services of Prince Leopold of Anhalt-Köthen. April 22: Bach elected Cantor of St Thomas's. May 5: Contract handed to Bach. May 22: Move to Leipzig. May 30: First performance in the Nicolaikirche. June 1: Introduction to his duties at the St Thomas's School. July 18: Funeral service for the wife of Postmaster Keess, and performance of the motet *Jesu meine Freude*. November 2: Dedication of the organ at Störmthal and performance of the cantata *Höchsterwünschtes Freudenfest*.

1724 Composition of numerous church cantatas.

1725 The second music book for Anna Magdalena Bach. Febuary 23: Performance of the secular cantata

Entfliehet, verschwindet, entweichet, ihr Sorgen, for the birthday of Duke Christian of Sachsen-Weissenfels. August 3: Performance of the *Aeolus-Kantate* on the saint's day of Professor August Friedrich Müller. September 20–21: Journey to Dresden and organ concert in the Sophienkirche there.

1726 November 30: Performance of a birthday cantata for the Princess of Köthen.

1727 October 17: Funeral service and performance of the ode in memory of the Elector's wife Christiane Eberhardine in the Paulinerkirche in Leipzig.

1728 February 5: Wedding cantata *Vergnügte Pleissenstadt*.

1729 Bach becomes director of Telemann's *collegium musicum*. February 23: Performance of birthday cantata for Duke Christian of Weissenfels. March 24: Performance of funeral cantata *Klagt, Kinder, klagt es aller Welt* for Prince Leopold in Köthen. April 15: Performance of the St Matthew Passion in the Thomaskirche in Leipzig. June: Vain attempt to meet Handel in Halle. October 24: Motet *Der Geist hilft unsrer Schwachheit auf* for the funeral service of Johann Heinrich Ernesti, deceased rector of St Thomas's.

1730 June 25–27: Festivities and performance of three Bach cantatas for the bicentenary of the Augsburg Confession. August 23: Project for a properly established church music. August 28: Letter to the friend of his early years, Georg Erdmann, in Danzig.

1731 The six clavier partitas appear in print as Op. 1, 'published by the author'. September 14: Organ concert in the Sophienkirche in Dresden.

1732 February: Organ-testing at Stönt-zsch. June 5: Inauguration of the enlarged building of the St Thomas school and performance of the cantata *Froher Tag, verlangte Stunden.* June 21: Birth of Bach's son Johann Christoph Friedrich. September 21: Journey to Kassel and organ-testing.

1733 February 1: Death of Friedrich August I – general mourning until July 2. July 27: The Kyrie and Gloria are sent to the court in Dresden. September 5: Performance of the cantata *Herkules auf dem Scheidewege* for the birthday of Prince Friedrich Christian. October 7: Performance of the cantata *Schleicht, spielende Wellen* for the birthday of Friedrich August II. December 8: Performance of the cantata *Tönet ihr Pauken* for the birthday of the Elector's wife Maria Josepha.

1734 August 3: Performance of the cantata *Auf, schmetternde Töne* for the saint's day of Friedrich August II. October 5: Performance of the cantata *Preise dein Glücke, gesegnetes Sachsen* for the anniversary of King Friedrich August II's election. November 21: Introduction of Johann August Ernesti, new rector of St Thomas's to his duties and performance of the cantata *Thomana sass annoch betrübt.*

1734–35 December 25 to January 6: Performance of the six parts of the Christmas Oratorio.

1735 June: Journey to Mühlhausen in the company of Johann Gottfried Bernhard Bach September 5: Birth of the son Johann Christian.

1736 'Musicalisches Gesang-Buch' – a book of hymns published by G. Chr. Schemelli with Bach as collaborator. August: Beginning of dispute over the appointment of a prefect. November 19: Bach is nominated composer to the court of Saxony. December 1: Concert in the Frauenkirche in Dresden on the Silbermann organ.

1737 October 18: Request to the Elector of Saxony for assistance in the dispute over the appointment of a prefect.

1738 April 27: Homage cantata *Willkommen, ihr herrschenden Götter der Erden* for Friedrich August II.

1739 September: Organ-testing at Altenburg.

1740 Carl Philipp Emanuel joins the chamber ensemble of Frederick II, King of Prussia, as cembalo player.

1741 August: Journey to Berlin and visit to Carl Philipp Emanuel.

1742 August 30: Performance of the *Bauern-kantate* on the estate at Kleinzschocher.

1743 March 11: Foundation of the 'Grosse Konzert' in Leipzig.

1744 The second part of the *Wohltemperirte Klavier.*

1745 November 10: Birth of Bach's first grandson, Johann August, son of Philipp Emanuel.

1746 August 7: Organ-testing at Zschortau. November 27: Organ-testing at Naumburg.

1747 May 7: Arrival at Potsdam. May 8: Organ recital in the Garnisonskirche. June: Elected member of the 'Society of Musical Sciences' in Leipzig. July 7: Despatch of the *Musical Offering* to Frederick II, King of Prussia.

1748 July 24: Bach recommends his pupil Altnikol for the post of organist at the Wenzel organ in Naumburg.

1749 Work on *The Art of Fugue*. January 20: Marriage of Bach's daughter Elisabeth Frederica to Johann Christoph Altnikol.

1750 March–April: Bach twice operated on by the English eye specialist John Taylor. July 28: Bach dies at a quarter to nine in the evening. July 31: Burial in the cemetery of St John.

NOTES ON THE PICTURES

Frontispiece: Johann Sebastian Bach; unsigned portrait in oils, presumably by Ernst Rentsch the Elder. This picture was painted when Bach was about 30 years old. (Städtisches Museum, Erfurt)

5 VIEW OF EISENACH, with the Wartburg in the background. After the engraving by Merian in 1650.

6 JOHANN AMBROSIUS BACH (1645–1695), Johann Sebastian's father who lived in Eisenach from 1671 as town and court musician. Unsigned oil-painting. (Deutsche Staatsbibliothek, Berlin)

7 THE 'BACH HOUSE' at the Frauenplan in Eisenach, now administered by the Bach Society. It is not certain whether the composer was born here. (Photo: Langematz)

BAPTISM of Johann Sebastian entered in the register of the Georgenkirche in Eisenach. (March 23, 1685)

8 EISENACH: Courtyard of the old Dominican monastery, home of the Latin school where Johann Sebastian was a pupil from his eighth year onwards. (Photo: Widmann)

9 THE ORGAN OF THE GEORGENKIRCHE in Eisenach designed by Johann Christoph Bach (1645–1693), Johann Sebastian's uncle. (Photo: Bachhaus Eisenach)

10 THE MICHAELISKIRCHE IN OHRDRUF where Johann Sebastian's eldest brother Johann Christoph Bach (1671–1721) was organist. The church was destroyed in 1945. (Photo: Stadtarchiv Ohrdruf)

11 VIEW OF OHRDRUF, after an engraving from the 'Codex diplomaticus Hohenlohicus 1753'.

12 LÜNEBURG: View of the town, after the engraving from Merian's Topographia of 1653.

13 ENTRY IN THE SCHOOL REGISTER of the Lyceum illustre Ordruviense, Classis II (1699). Bach's name appears as No. 2. His name appears again in the lower column with a remark saying that no free place could be found for him at this school, and that he left for Lüneburg in 1700: 'Lüneburgum ob defectum hospitiorum se contulit die 15 Martii 1700'. (Stadtarchiv Ohrdruf)

AN ACCOUNT OF PAYMENTS TO CHORISTERS of the Michaelisschule in Lüneburg, dated May 29, 1700. Bach's name is the ninth on the list. He was a member of the choir from 1700 to 1702. (Michaeliskloster-Archiv, Lüneburg)

14 MICHAELISKIRCHE, LÜNEBURG: View of the nave, after a painting by Joachim Burmester. (After 1700; Museum Lüneburg)

15 JAN ADAMS REINKEN (1623–1722), born in the Netherlands, was one of the most famous organists of his time. He worked for many years at the Katharinenkirche in Hamburg. After an unsigned oil-painting. (Museum für Hamburgische Geschichte)

16 THE NEUE KIRCHE AT ARNSTADT. In July 1703 Bach came to this church to test the organ built by J. Fr. Wender between 1699 and 1703. He became organist there on August 9, 1703. (Charcoal drawing: Georg Renger)

17 THE PALACE AT CELLE to which Bach often went from Lüneburg, hoping to learn something from the performances given by its court orchestra. Drawing by G. Siebers printed by A. H. Oetling (c. 1830), Bomann-Museum, Celle.

19 ORGANIST'S SEAT AND CONSOLE of the old Bach organ, now preserved in the Bach memorial at Arnstadt. (Photo: Ruhe)

20 RECEIPT for 18 florins, 15 groschen and 9 pfennigs signed by Bach on June 15, 1707. Several such receipts are in existence from the composer's days in Arnstadt. (Stadtarchiv Arnstadt)

21 PORTAL OF THE MARIENKIRCHE in Mühlhausen. The cantata for the inauguration of the new council was performed here on February 4, 1708.

22 VILLAGE CHURCH AT DORNHEIM. Johann Sebastian and Maria Barbara Bach, his cousin, were married by the parson Lorenz Stauber in this church on October 17, 1707, shortly after leaving Arnstadt for Mühlhausen. (Charcoal drawing: Georg Renger)

24 CANTATA *Gott ist mein König*. Text and parts of this cantata for the inauguration of the new council were printed on behalf of the civic authorities. The plates show the title page and the first text page. (Deutsche Staatsbibliothek, Berlin)

25 SCORE of the cantata *Gott ist mein König* in Bach's handwriting; last page. (Deutsche Staatsbibliothek, Berlin)

27 NEW BACH ORGAN in the Blasiuskirche at Mühlhausen where Bach became organist on June 15, 1707. The organ was in need of repair; it was renovated to the composer's detailed specifications. It was replaced by an inferior instrument in 1821. In 1958–59 A. Schuke (Potsdam) reconstructed the organ shown on this plate according to Bach's design. (Photo: Sawade)

28 JOHANN ADOLPH FROHNE (1652–1713), Superintendent at Mühlhausen. As follower of the Pietists, he opposed the use of concerted music in the divine service. Frohne was Bach's immediate superior at Mühlhausen. (Unsigned oil-painting, Superintendentur Mühlhausen)

GEORG CHRISTIAN EILMAR (1665–1715), vicar of the Marienkirche in Mühlhausen, who supported Bach in the quarrel over the use of music in church. (Unsigned oil-painting, Superintendentur Mühlhausen)

29 BACH'S REQUEST FOR DISMISSAL (part of last page), written to the council on June 25, 1708. The request was granted one day later. (Stadtarchiv Mühlhausen)

30 VIEW OF WEIMAR after the engraving by G. M. Kraus (18th century).

31 DUKE WILHELM ERNST of Sachsen-Weimar (1662–1728) employed Johann Sebastian in 1708 as member of the chamber music ensemble and court organist. (Portrait by Pieter Schenk. Staatliche Kunstsammlungen Weimar)

32 THE CHURCH OF SS. PETER AND PAUL, WEIMAR. Johann Gottfried Walther (1684–1748), cousin and close friend of Johann Sebastian, was organist at the old Stadtkirche in Weimar. (After the engraving by A. Alboth)

MUSICALISCHES LEXIKON by J. G. Walther, published 1732 in Leipzig.

It was the first musical publication to discuss Johann Sebastian Bach.

33 MUSIKALISCHES LEXIKON by J. G. Walther, (1732); frontispiece depicting a contemporary concert

34 THE WILHELMSBURG, palace of Duke Wilhelm Ernst of Sachsen-Weimar, and the main centre of musical activities in Weimar during Bach's stay in this town. After the engraving by Christian and Wilhelm Richter (1654)

35 ERNST AUGUST, Prince of Sachsen-Weimar (1688–1748), nephew of Wilhelm Ernst the ruling Duke of Sachsen-Weimar, lived with his mother and his brother Johann Ernst in the 'Rote Schloss'. Bach often made music with the two Princes until the Duke forbade him to do so. (Unsigned painting, Staatliche Kunstsammlugen, Weimar)

36 ARCANGELO CORELLI (1653–1713), Italian composer. Lithograph by Maurin the Elder. (Deutsche Staatsbibliothek Berlin)

37 ANTONIO VIVALDI (1675–1741), Italian composer. Engraving by Lambert the Younger. (Deutsche Staatsbibliothek Berlin)

38 THE SCHLOSSKIRCHE IN WEIMAR, called the 'Himmelsburg' (castle of heaven), after the renovation of 1658. The church was burnt down in 1774. After a painting of Christian Richter, about 1660. (Staatliche Kunstsammlungen, Weimar)

40 VIEW OF HALLE, after the engraving from 'Views of 93 famous towns', Leipzig 1746. (Deutsche Staatsbibliothek Berlin)

41 AUTOGRAPH SCORE by Bach. Beginning of the aria 'Christi Glieder, ach bedenket', from the cantata Bereitet die Wege, bereitet die Bahn. (Now in the Universitätsbibliothek Tübingen)

43 CHRISTIAN, Duke of Sachsen-Weissenfels (1682–1736). The Jagdkantate was performed at Weissenfels for the Duke's birthday in February 1716. (Oil-painting, Stadtmuseum Weissenfels)

ERDMANN NEUMEISTER (1671–1756), parson in Hamburg, brought new life into church music by introducing operatic elements into his texts. (After an engraving in the Deutsche Staatsbibliothek Berlin)

44 JAGDKANTATE, beginning of the aria 'Weil die wollenreichen Herden' in Bach's handwriting. (Deutsche Staatsbibliothek Berlin)

45 BACH'S SIGNATURE for a testimonial dated April 4, 1731. On this occasion he used the title of 'Capellmeister to the court of Weissenfels'.

46 THE ORGELBÜCHLEIN OF WEIMAR. Choral prelude 'Liebster Jesu, wir sind hier'. Autograph. (Deutsche Staatsbibliothek Berlin)

47 LOUIS MARCHAND (1669–1732), French keyboard virtuoso, agreed to a musical contest with Bach during the autumn of 1717, but failed to appear. (Engraving by Charles Dupuis after a painting by Jean Robert; Kupferstichkabinett Dresden/Deutsche Fotothek Dresden)

48 THE CASTLE AT KÖTHEN, after the engraving from Merian's Topographia of 1650.

49 JOHANN SEBASTIAN BACH, portrait by Johann Jakob Ihle (about 1720). (Bachhaus Eisenach)

50 PRINCE LEOPOLD of Anhalt-Köthen (1694/1728) became Bach's employer in 1717. Part of an unsigned painting. (Köthen, privately owned)

51 BIRTHDAY SERENADE for Prince Leopold of Anhalt-Köthen, 1717.

Autograph. (Deutsche Staatsbibliothek Berlin)

53 COURTYARD OF THE CASTLE AT KÖTHEN, Ludwigsbau. (Photo: Schmähmann)

54 SONATA FOR SOLO VIOLIN in A minor. First movement, Grave. Autograph. (Now in the Universitätsbibliothek Tübingen)

55 CHRISTIAN LUDWIG, Margrave of Brandenburg (1677–1734), received from Bach six *concerts avec plusieurs instruments* (1721), which were named after him the *Brandenburg Concertos*. Engraving by Bernigeroth. (Staatliche Museen Berlin, Kupferstichkabinett)

56/7 SIXTH BRANDENBURG CONCERTO in B flat major. Beginning of the first movement. Autograph. (Deutsche Staatsbibliothek Berlin)

59 CLAVIERBÜCHLEIN for Wilhelm Friedemann Bach (1710–1784). On January 22, 1720 Bach began to write for his son one of the best keyboard tutors.

60 TWO-PART INVENTIONS, autograph title page; 1723. (Deutsche Staatsbibliothek Berlin)

61 TWO-PART INVENTIONS, beginning of the fourteenth invention. Autograph. (Deutsche Staatsbibliothek Berlin)

62 THE WOHLTEMPERIRTE CLAVIER, title page. This collection of 24 preludes and fugues in all the keys is to this day one of the basic contrapuntal works. Autograph. (Deutsche Staatsbibliothek Berlin)

63 THE WOHLTEMPERIRTE CLAVIER (1722), beginning of the E major Fugue. Autograph. (Deutsche Staatsbibliothek Berlin)

64 VIEW OF KARLSBAD, after the engraving of Joseph Spahn (about 1730). (Deutsche Staatsbibliothek Berlin)

VIEW OF HAMBURG, after the engraving by J. B. Homann (about 1720). (Deutsche Staatsbibliothek Berlin)

65 ORGAN BY ARP SCHNITGER in the Jakobikirche in Hamburg. The post of organist was vacant in this church when Bach visited Hamburg in November 1720, but he returned to Köthen without having applied for it. (Museum für Hamburgische Geschichte, Archiv)

66 MUSIC BOOK FOR ANNA MAGDALENA BACH (1725), aria 'Bist Du bei mir'. The first of these *Notenbüchlein* was made by Bach in 1722. (Now in the Westdeutsche Bibliothek Marburg)

68 HANDWRITING OF ANNA MAGDALENA BACH, the composer's second wife. Third Suite for Cello. (Now in the Universitätsbibliothek Tübingen)

69 FRIEDERIKA HENRIETTA, Princess of Anhalt-Köthen. After the engraving by J. C. G. Fritsch (1756). (Heimatmuseum Köthen)

70 VIEW OF LEIPZIG (about 1720), engraving by J. G. Ringlin after a drawing by F. B. Werner. (Bach-Archiv Leipzig)

71 JOHANN KUHNAU (1660–1722), Bach's predecessor as cantor of St Thomas's, here portrayed on the title page of his 'Neue Clavir-Übung' (1689). (Musikbibliothek Leipzig)

72 GEORG PHILIPP TELEMANN (1681–1767), Kapellmeister and famous composer at Hamburg, was the most likely candidate for the post of cantor of St Thomas's after Kuhnau's death. Telemann was elected unanimously on August 11, 1722, but he

returned to Hamburg where, after some hesitation, he decided to remain, having obtained an increase in his salary. (Deutsche Staatsbibliothek Berlin)

73 CHRISTOPH GRAUPNER (1683–1760) Kapellmeister in the service of the Prince of Hessen-Darmstadt, with Bach the only other serious candidate after Telemann's refusal. Graupner was elected, but since his employer would not release him, he wrote in a letter of March 22, 1723 that he was forced to decline the offer. Graupner's signature and the end of this letter are shown on p. 73. (Stadtarchiv Leipzig)

74/75 UNDERTAKING, dated April 19, 1723, in which Bach had to assure the Leipzig council of his goodwill and readiness to do his duty according to the rules of the school of St Thomas, even before his election. (Stadtarchiv Leipzig)

76 CONTRACT, last page. This document was handed to Bach and signed on May 5, 1723. The document contained a pedantically detailed list of all his duties. (Stadtarchiv Leipzig)

77 SALOMON DEYLING (1677–1755), Superintendent and Bach's immediate superior for 27 years. (Unsigned oil-painting in the choir of the Thomaskirche. Photo: Knoll)

78 LIST OF TEACHERS AT THE SCHOOL OF ST THOMAS for 1723. Kuhnau's name appears in the margin. (Stadtarchiv Leipzig)

RECEIPT for the fee for testing an organ in Leipzig on December 18, 1717 for the University; evidence of Bach's first appearance in the city. (Universitätsarchiv Leipzig)

79 THE THOMASKIRCHE IN LEIPZIG, seen from the north. After a lithograph by Strassberger. (Early 19th century)

80 TOWN PLAN OF LEIPZIG published in 1723 by Matth. Seutter in Augsburg. (Stadtgeschichtliches Museum Leipzig)

81 CHURCH AND SCHOOL OF ST THOMAS in 1723. Engraving by J. G. Krügner for the frontispiece of the 'Rules and regulations for the school of St Thomas 1723'. (Bach-Archiv Leipzig)

82 THE MARKET SQUARE OF LEIPZIG. Engraving of J. G. Schreiber (1712). (Bach-Archiv Leipzig)

83 THE THOMASPFÖRTCHEN, or little St Thomas gate, with church and school. After an engraving by G. B. Probst. (Bach-Archiv Leipzig)

84 SCHOOL OF ST THOMAS and Thomaspförtchen, after an illustration from the 'Musikalisches Wochenblatt', 35th year of publication, No. 40 (1904). In 1902 the old school-building was demolished. The Bach memorial in the foreground on the left was presented and dedicated by Felix Mendelssohn-Bartholdy in 1843.

MEMORIAL PLAQUE for the old school of St Thomas, put up in 1935 but melted down after a few years.

85 THE NICOLAIKIRCHE IN LEIPZIG in Bach's time, after the engraving by J. Stridbeck. On May 30, 1723 the composer performed his first cantata *Die Elenden sollen essen* in this principal church of the city. (Stadtgeschichtliches Museum Leipzig)

86 BACH'S SIGNATURE on a testimonial of May 18, 1727.

GROUPING OF THE CHOIR. A note in Bach's hand with the division of his choristers into four groups. (Stadtarchiv Leipzig)

87 PART OF BACH'S PLAN for a properly established church music, with re-

marks on the use of his choristers for the various church services. Autograph. (Bach-Archiv Leipzig)

88 TESTIMONIAL BY BACH for the journeyman town piper Carl Friedrich Pfaffe, written on July 24, 1745. Autograph. (Stadtarchiv Leipzig)

TESTIMONIAL BY BACH for Johann Christoph Altnikol, his future son-in-law, written on May 25, 1747. Autograph. (Bach-Archiv Leipzig)

89 INTERIOR OF THE THOMASKIRCHE before 1885. Engraving by Kutschers after a watercolour by H. Kratz. (Bach-Archiv Leipzig)

90 GOTTFRIED REICHE (1667–1734), a trumpeter in the 'Leipzig Municipal Orchestra' and the best wind player at Bach's disposal. He died on October 6, 1734 because he had strained himself while playing for the King's election the previous night. Painting by E. G. Haussmann, about 1725. (Stadtgeschichtliches Museum Leipzig)

91 FLUTE PART of an aria from the cantata No. 101. Autograph. (Bach-Archiv Leipzig)

92 MASS IN A MAJOR: 'Fine. Soli Deo Gloria'. (End. To God alone be praise.)

93 JOHANN HEINRICH ERNESTI, rector of St Thomas's from 1684 to 1729. After an engraving by Bernigeroth. (Stadtgeschichtliches Museum Leipzig)

95 PAULINERKIRCHE IN LEIPZIG. Music at this church was in Bach's opinion his responsibility, the University authorities did not agree and a long dispute ensued. Coloured drawing by Benjamin Schwarz. (Bach-Archiv Leipzig)

97 CHRISTIANE EBERHARDINE (1671–1727), Queen of Poland and wife of the Elector of Saxony, Friedrich August I (1670 to 1733). Engraving. (Artist unknown.) 1728.

JOHANN CHRISTOPH GOTTSCHED (1700 to 1766). Oil-painting by L. Schorer, 1744. (Stadtbibliothek Leipzig)

FUNERAL ODE for Christiane Eberhardine, 1727. Title page of Bach's autograph score. (Deutsche Staatsbibliothek Berlin)

98 RECEIPT IN BACH'S HANDWRITING of May 5, 1738 for 58 thalers, being the fee for the homage cantata *Willkommen, ihr herrschenden Götter der Erden*. (Universitätsarchiv Leipzig)

99 FRIEDRICH AUGUST II (1696–1763), Elector of Saxony, and from 1733 King Augustus III of Poland. For the anniversary of his election Bach wrote the festive cantata *Preise dein Glücke, gesegnetes Sachsen* (engraving unsigned, 1737).

100 GLORIA OF THE B MINOR MASS, end of the bass part in Bach's handwriting. (Landesbibliothek Dresden)

101 LETTER BY BACH, dated July 27, 1733, accompanying the parts of the *B minor Mass* which he sent to the court in Dresden. The original, formerly in the Landesbibliothek Dresden, was destroyed during the Second World War.

102 JOHANN MATTHIAS GESNER, rector of St Thomas's from 1730 to 1734, knew Bach from his Weimar days and supported him in his quarrels with the Leipzig authorities. Painting by E. G. Haussmann. (school of St Thomas Leipzig)

103 CANON for J. M. Gesner, dated January 10, 1734.

104 PETITION by Bach, dated August 12, 1736, defending his right to a vote in the election of a choir prefect. (Stadtarchiv Leipzig)

105 JOHANN AUGUST ERNESTI, rector of St Thomas's from 1734 to 1759. Although well disposed towards Bach at first, he later tried to limit the cantor's freedom as a composer. A violent dispute broke out between the two men in 1736. Oil-painting by Anton Graff (school of St Thomas, Leipzig)

106/7 CHRISTMAS ORATORIO. Title page and beginning of the 'libretto' of 1734. (Lent to the Bach-Archiv Leipzig by the Musikbibliothek Leipzig)

108 PHILIPP EMANUEL BACH (1714–1788). In 1740, cembalo player in the service of Frederick the Great, King of Prussia. In 1768 he succeeded Telemann as musical director of the five main Hamburg churches. (Portrait in pastels, about 1732 to 33, probably by Samuel Anton Bach. Bachhaus Eisenach)

109 WILHELM FRIEDEMANN BACH (1710–1784). In 1733, organist at the Sophienkirche in Dresden, 1746 at the Liebfrauenkirche in Halle. (Portraits in pastels, about 1732/33, probably by Samuel Anton Bach. Bachhaus Eisenach)

110/111 VIEW OF DRESDEN, after the engraving by Schlitterlan, about 1740. (Deutsche Staatsbibliothek Berlin)

112 THE SILBERMANN organ in the Sophienkirche, Dresden, where Bach gave a recital in 1731. His son Wilhelm Friedemann became organist there in 1733. (Deutsche Fotothek Dresden)

113 THE SILBERMANN organ in the Frauenkirche, Dresden, finished in 1736. Soon afterwards Bach gave a concert there on the occasion of his appointment as composer to the court of Saxony. (Deutsche Fotothek Dresden)

114 THE FRAUENKIRCHE IN DRESDEN, after the etching by Canaletto (1757).

CLAVIR-ÜBUNG I (1731), title page of the first edition of 1731. (Musikbibliothek Leipzig)

117 JOHANN SEBASTIAN BACH, oil-painting by E. G. Haussmann, 1746. (Stadtgeschichtliches Museum Leipzig)

118 FRIEDRICH II (1712–1786). Frederick the Great, King of Prussia, after the engraving by J. Kleinschmidt. (Berlin, Kupferstichkabinett)

119 KEYBOARD INSTRUMENT BY SILBERMANN of 1746 in the palace of Sanssouci at Potsdam. (Photo: Verwaltung der Staatlichen Schlösser und Gärten, Potsdam)

120 MUSICAL OFFERING, Canon perpetuus super Thema regium, from the first edition of 1747. (Deutsche Staatsbibliothek Berlin)

121 THE ART OF FUGUE. Last page of the score in Bach's handwriting. A note of Carl Philipp Emanuel says that the composer died when he had introduced the notes BACH (see footnote on p. 34) in the counter-subject (Deutsche Staatsbibliothek Berlin)

123 PETITION BY ANNA MAGDALENA BACH, dated October 21, 1750. Having declared that she has no intention of remarrying, she assumes full responsibility for her young children. (Sächsisches Landeshauptarchiv Dresden)

124 SARCOPHAGUS WITH THE COMPOSER'S REMAINS in the Johanniskirche in Leipzig (until 1949).

142

INDEX OF NAMES

Numbers in italics refer to the illustrations